CARS EUROPE NEVER BUILT

FIFTY YEARS OF EXPERIMENTAL CARS

Gregory Janicki

Sterling Publishing Co., Inc.   New York

Library of Congress Cataloging-in-Publication Data

Janicki, Gregory.
    Cars Europe never built / by Gregory Janicki.
        p.   cm.
    Includes index.
    ISBN 0-8069-8592-5
    1. Experimental automobiles—Europe—History.   I. Title.
TL55.J36   1992
629.222—dc20   92–19126
                                     CIP

Design and layout by David Levy

Photo credits: Archivio Perini—1988 Michelotti Pura; *Automobile Quarterly*—1933 Jaray BMW 2-Liter, 1934 Jaray Audi Front; Bill Bailey; Giorgio Bella—1960 Pininfarina X, 1969 Ferrari 512S, 1981 Audi Quartz, 1989 Ferrari Mythos, 1991 Pininfarina Chronos; British Motor Industry Trust—1961 Rover Turbine; Carrozzeria Bertone; Italdesign; Mercedes-Benz Museum; Pininfarina Archives; Porsche Archives; and Quadrant Picture Library—1946 Mathis 333, 1948 Brandt

10 9 8 7 6 5 4 3 2 1

Published by Sterling Publishing Company, Inc.
387 Park Avenue South, New York, N.Y. 10016
© 1992 by Gregory Janicki
Distributed in Canada by Sterling Publishing
℅ Canadian Manda Group, P.O. Box 920, Station U
Toronto, Ontario, Canada M8Z 5P9
Distributed in Great Britain and Europe by Cassell PLC
Villiers House, 41/47 Strand, London WC2N 5JE, England
Distributed in Australia by Capricorn Link Ltd.
P.O. Box 665, Lane Cove, NSW 2066
Printed and bound in Hong Kong
Sterling ISBN 0-8069-8592-5

ACKNOWLEDGMENTS

This book could not have been completed without the assistance of many people. Thanks, Dad. It's all because of you. Thank you, Maria, my wife, for helping me through (and putting up with) the long computer-clicking nights, photo-organizing days, and stress-filled months. You are the greatest. Thanks to my family: Mom, Michael, Donna, Cheryl, Kellie, Amanda, and Mom and Dad Dolinski. And thanks to all my friends who knew better than to call me during the last days.

Special thanks to: the ASQ Corporation and staff (Mac, Joe, and Kelly) for their patience and understanding; Autograph AB for their European hospitality; Jorgen Malmgren for the prompt translations; Nakamura-san for the Frankfurt introductions; Edward Bornoty for the trips to the library and sympathetic telephone conversations; Jerry McDermott for the photos, information, time, and support; Dick Lilley for introducing me to Jerry; Anne Hope for the information; Craig Cather and the German office for the translations; Ronald Grantz and the staff at the National Automotive History Collection at the Detroit Public Library; Gerry Wallerstein; Stig Borklund; Steve Stringer; Paul Lienert; Dean Case; Bill Bailey; and Lance Benaton.

Grateful acknowledgment to the following people and companies for photos and information. I could not have done it without you: the Janicki basement archives; Lorenza Pininfarina of Industrie Pininfarina S.p.A.; Lorenza Cappello and Fabrizio Giugiaro of Italdesign; Donna Reichle of Fiat; Franco Sbarro of Ateliers de Constructions Automobiles Sbarro; Robert Mitchell and Valarie Kalbouch of BMW of North America; Maria Leonhauser and Tony Fouladpour of Volkswagen, United States, Inc.; Craig Morningstar and Renaldo Hercolani of Alfa Romeo; Judith Nitsche of Audi AG; Maureen Moreland of Audi of America, Inc.; Susanne Hutter of Porsche AG; Anders Turnberg of SAAB; George Ryder and Denise Kaiser of Pininfarina USA; Gian Beppe Panicco of Carrozzeria Bertone S.p.A.; Andrew Marshall of Adam Opel AG; John Chuhran of Mercedes-Benz of North America; Martin Alloiteau of Automobiles Peugeot; Thore Lodin of Volvo Cars AB; Carolyn Reimann of Range Rover of North America; Michael Kennedy and Elaine Winterburn of Rover Cars; Jerry Duller of Vauxhall Motors Ltd.; Gro Hoeg of Citroën; Regie Nationale des Usines Renault; Gert Pollmann of G. Pollmann; Harry Niemann Mercedes-Benz Museum; Lef Lawrence and Lynn Duffin of IAD; Grazia Bergagna of Ghia S.p.A.; Mrs. Maury of Matra; Christian Garnier-Collot of Design Volanis, and Roger Stowers of Aston Martin Lagonda Ltd.

CONTENTS

INTRODUCTION

Everyone has an interest in the future. Ask thirty people and you're likely to get thirty different answers on what's ahead for the next two, five or fifty years. Some of these predictions will seem to be the general consensus, others completely ridiculous (sometimes the general consensus is completely ridiculous), but all will share one common characteristic: they will all be guesses—some educated, some ignorant. Some of these predictions do become reality. Unfortunately, as anyone who has planned a weekend vacation around the latest weather report can attest, no prediction is foolproof. Right or wrong, though, the guessing game continues.

Cars Europe Never Built is a collection of automotive guesses—a mixed bag of vehicle design exercises that speculated on the future of the automobile. Some of the ideas presented in these experiments found a home on a production vehicle. Others only lasted the length of the auto show circuit. But in each instance, the vehicle was one company's view of the future.

Over the years, these futuristic automobile designs have addressed a variety of areas. The most investigated area was, and still is, aerodynamics—the reason being that aerodynamics affect both the technical aspects of the vehicle (fuel economy, brake cooling, etc.) and its stylistic aspects. In fact, to quite a few people, the most important byproduct of aerodynamic study is the stunning shape created.

Although aerodynamic experimentation goes back to the inception of the automobile itself, *Cars Europe Never Built* begins with the sleek, somewhat anachronistic curves and angles from the 1930s that set the stage for the post-war boom in vehicle design. The creative liberation after World War II engendered countless styles beginning with the integration of the wheels into the car's body in an attempt to create a sleeker vehicle. The 1950s saw wings, fins, curves and the occasional egg shape, as designers strove for faster vehicles. The wedge profile appeared on the automotive scene in the 1960s as aerodynamics became more scientific with increased wind-tunnel testing. The late 1960s and early 1970s brought some of the most fanciful designs ever—for aerodynamic reasons as well as for pure publicity. Also in the 1970s and early 1980s a more realistic approach to exterior experimental design emerged as carmakers struggled with the effect of two major fuel crises. Sleek vehicles took on a more pragmatic purpose than simply speed: fuel economy. This period also expanded the use of plastics and non-sheet-metal bodies formed to increase fuel economy through decreased weight. The 1990s have begun with an effort to combine the wild and functional with sleek vehicle bodies masking powerful engines that produce less pollutants.

The perfect aerodynamic form? A single answer doesn't exist simply because the purpose of the automobile dictates its form. A narrow, flat, zero-headroom car design may cut the air with minimum resistance, but don't try fitting a family of five into it.

Vehicle experimentation also falls into four other loosely related categories: alternative power sources, safety, new technology and the purely wild.

Experimentation with alternative power sources for the automobile—alternative, that is, to the internal combustion engine—also has a long history. In today's environment-conscious society, the search for the environment-friendly automobile has taken on greater importance and manufacturers allot millions of dollars to study unusual forms of power generation. Gas turbine power was the hope of the future during the 1950s and 1960s. Electric propulsion appeared early on in the history of the automotive industry and continues to hold the greatest attention today. Whatever the choice, it's certain that these vehicles will be revealed to the public in the form of an experimental vehicle.

Another area of experimentation is safety. It was 20 years ago that the first air bag and motorized seat belt were tested in an experimental vehicle. Fifty years have passed since exterior designs with pedestrian safety in mind emerged. Stacks of test vehicles have been crashed, dropped, probed, and otherwise manipulated—all so that the public would have safer transportation.

New technology encompasses features like automatic speed-sensitive spoilers and head-up displays, as well as other interior gadgets that have slowly found their way to either the production vehicle or the trash bin. Navigation systems and rear-mounted cameras are easing into today's production vehicles, but the high-tech parking-ticket holder has yet to find itself on a vehicle option list.

The purely wild category comprises the "show stoppers," the vehicles everyone went home talking about. These vehicles combined elements of all the aforementioned categories into one pure fantasy vehicle. Mostly utilized as promotional tools, these vehicles tested the public's acceptance to a bulbous fender, a steeply raked windshield, or an unorthodox seating arrangement. The designer, allowed to guess, or better yet, "play," without marketing plans or managerial breath on the back of his neck, thus created a product that would make a grown man weep because he either (1) knew he couldn't have it or (2) thought the rear spoiler was simply hideous.

Cars Europe Never Built outlines the many design themes emphasized at various points in time as carmakers and designers attempted to balance the current social and economic climate with future goals. That process has not been an easy trick. Today's designer must look where he's been to see where he's going; he must analyze what worked and what didn't work to develop vehicles that can be produced economically and, more important, that appeal to the consumer. Today this means a vehicle that possesses good fuel economy, a comfortable interior, and adequate acceleration while it treats the environment with kid gloves. Any questions about the value of a one-of-a-kind concept or experimental vehicles built to address these requirements, with designers "guessing" whether a certain innovation will catch on, are simply answered: "Does anyone have a better answer?"

And typically, the only answer comes from another manufacturer who has its own ideas of the future and how its plan is better—or so it guesses.

JARAY EXPERIMENTS

One of the most significant contributors to the early science of automobile aerodynamics was Austrian-born Paul Jaray. A mathematician by trade, Jaray experimented first with lighter-than-air zeppelins before turning to automobiles in 1921. Utilizing his mathematical calculations and a wind tunnel in Germany (built in 1917), Jaray designed a vehicle in 1922 that achieved a coefficient of drag of 0.245. Low by today's standards; unbelievable for 1922.

The two vehicles pictured here, the 1933 Audi Front (which Jaray used as personal transportation until the 1950s) and the 1934 BMW 2 liter, exemplify the integrated designs of Paul Jaray: a high stance (the high chassis of the day necessitated this), a rounded windshield, and smooth bumpers. The latter design cue signaled another advanced design trait of Jaray's—safety. The rounder a vehicle, the less harm would be inflicted on a pedestrian upon collision. Another unique characteristic of the Jaray vehicle was a flap situated in the middle of the panoramic windshield that provided excellent ventilation.

Although his concepts found little application in the 1920s and 1930s (only one company, the Czechoslovakian firm Tatra, actually mass-produced a Jaray-designed vehicle in 1934, the Tatra 77), his practice of streamlining the whole automobile rather than singling out such parts as headlights and door handles lives in today's vehicle designs.

LANCIA APRILIA

Battista "Pinin" Farina, the founder of the Italian coachbuilding giant Pininfarina, was one of the early proponents of aerodynamics—or streamlining, as it was called back then—as applied to automobiles. Between the two world wars, Pininfarina experimented with styles quite out of the ordinary in search of the perfect form. The Lancia Aprilia was an eye-catching vehicle, especially for 1936, with its covered wheels, rounded windshield, and sharply sloped rear. Many of these design themes were simultaneously explored by the Austrian mathematician Paul Jaray. Pininfarina experimented on a variety of Lancia chassis during the 1930s, running the streamlined cars up hills and down Italian roads. Top speed for the vehicles reached 100 mph. Pininfarina went on to experiment further with aerodynamic shapes after World War II. The 1960 "X" represented the ideal aerodynamic shape for Pininfarina: the egg.

MATHIS 333

The three-wheel Mathis 333 of 1946 qualifies more as a production failure than an experimental car. Built with every intent to mass-produce, the Mathis never received production approval from the French government.

The name of the egg-shaped 333 was derived from the number of wheels, seats, and the 3 liter per 100 kilometer (79 mpg) fuel economy. Power for the Mathis originated from a 700 cc flat twin-power engine driving the independently sprung front wheels. Weight of the vehicle was a mere 840 pounds.

Another Mathis vehicle was introduced in 1948 with a flat six 2.8 liter engine, a panoramic windshield, and four wheels. Though a bit more conventional in wheel placement, the 1948 Mathis never reached the consumer. In 1954 the Mathis plant was sold to Citroën. The last Mathis to actually reach the public was built in 1935.

BRANDT

The French-built Brandt of 1948 has been described as one of the most unconventional cars of post–World War II. No argument here. At the heart of its unconventional appearance was the door placement. *Sans* side doors, entrance to the vehicle was gained through either the front or rear. Opening the large front door, which incorporated the windshield, revealed a gangway that bisected the interior and forced the four passengers to sit on either side. The Brandt was powered by a 985 cc horizontal engine which drove the front wheels. All four wheels were somewhat covered with rounded, two-tone bodywork. Headlights? One can only guess that the narrow objects protruding from the front bumpers provided some sort of illumination. Or then again, maybe that's the vehicle's rear. Needless to say, the Brandt never reached the production line.

PORSCHE TYPE 530 4-SEATER

Not very long after the 356 went into production in 1948 Porsche began to experiment with a four-seat version of the 2+2 356 coupe. In 1951 and 1952 two prototypes were built on a 94.5-inch wheelbase: a coupe and a cabriolet. The vehicles were designated type 530. The coupe had a notchback design and the cabriolet had wraparound bumpers. The doors on both vehicles were enlarged to accommodate entrance and exit for the rear passengers. The rear seats could also fold down for increased luggage capacity.

Although the vehicles did not fall into the dream car category—they were built with production goals—a 356 4-seater never went beyond the experimental stage (Porsche cited marketing reasons) and thus falls into the "never were" category.

To this day Porsche continues to experiment with the expanded interior and exterior theme, with a rumored four-door (yes, that's four-door) coming into production possibly around 1997. Look out, Mercedes-Benz.

PEGASO THRILL BERLINETTA

Thrill Berlinetta: What an inspired name for a sports car. Actually, the Spanish vehicle's official full birth name was the Pegaso 102/B Thrill Touring Berlinetta. Somehow the former rolls off the tongue better.

Quite a few Pegasos were constructed with special bodies by Carrozeria Touring in Italy and Saoutchik in France. The Thrill was bodied by Touring. One of the best known Pegasos, the Thrill was exhibited in many European car shows and even reached the cover of *Road and Track* in November 1954. The car pictured here—chassis 0133—is the sole example of this particular body style. The engine was a ninety-degree 2.8 liter V8.

Approximately eighty-five Pegasos were built in the 1950s as sports car production ceased, to make room for expanded production of heavy trucks.

ALFA ROMEO BAT 5, 7 & 9

Although these three prototypes had a resemblance to the nocturnal flying creature, the BAT actually stood for "Berlina Aerodynamica Tecnica" (or "streamlined closed touring car"). Built on an Alfa Romeo 1900 chassis with bodies by Bertone, BAT 5, 7 & 9 were developmental prototypes constructed to study the effects of tail wings on vehicle stability; they also served as experiments in pure aerodynamics.

The 1953 BAT 5 featured wheels enclosed to just below hub-line. The tail fins were curved in. Top speed was 123 mph, a 15 percent increase over the standard-production Alfa Romeo 1900. Coefficient of drag was reduced by 38 percent. Air was fed through the radiator from small slots in the front, moved through the wheel houses and exited via vaned side grilles behind the front wheels.

The 1954 BAT 7 featured the evolution of a more aircraft-like nose. The tail fins were more dramatically curved and the doors were deeply recessed for increased airflow from the front wheel slots.

The BAT 9 of 1955 was somewhat close to the production Alfa Romeo 2000. The tail fins were de-emphasized for better rear visibility and the more traditional Alfa front grille returned. The headlamps were behind plastic covers.

All three vehicles were brought to the U.S. by Stanley Harold "Wacky" Arnold and eventually sold.

1 9 5 4

FIAT 8001 TURBINE

In 1948 Fiat set out to develop a gas turbine engine for automobile use. The result was the Fiat 8001 Turbine of 1954. Based on a Fiat V8 Sport chassis, the Fiat Turbine was a long-appearing vehicle with a wind-tunnelled honed drag coefficient of 0.14.

The front mouth-like grille funnelled air to the turbine. Hot air was expelled from the huge jet-like rear exhaust. The painted quasi-flames on each side and two huge wings—huge even by Cadillac standards—hinted at an unusual power source. The over-size tires and wheel arches gave the vehicle a race-like appearance. Doors were opened against the wind. The vehicle had no transmission and the only controls were steering, throttle, and brake.

As with many other turbines of their day (Renault, Rover, Chrysler, General Motors, etc.) the Fiat tests ended in disappointment. In 1954, after six years of research, the project was shelved.

ALFA ROMEO 6C 3500 SUPERFLOW I

A true styling exercise—Pininfarina completed few "exercises" in the early days, concentrating on one-offs sold to private buyers—the Superflow displayed some interesting features, some more functional than others.

Presented at the 1956 Turin show, the gull-wing-type Superflow I appeared incomplete because it was. Executed in a very short time for the show, the Superflow had a rough-cut front wheel well covered in plexiglass that served as a streamliner for the pop-up headlights. The design was a unique approach to the nascent technology of aerodynamics. The side windows and a blue-tinted removable plastic roof were distinctive in that the metal portion of the door opened out while the windows flipped up. Inside, the instrument panel—which held only two round gauges set one on top of the other—and other interior projections were padded. A large central tunnel separated the two occupants.

The Superflow II debut later in 1956 was with a more finished appearance: solid fenders, and a duck-bill-like front sans the Alfa grille. The plastic did reappear in the rear fins and the covered headlights.

The overall shape of the Superflows was a forerunner to the Alfa Romeo Duetto Spider with the large body-side groove remaining.

ALFA ROMEO 2000 SPORTIVA

The Bertone-bodied Sportiva was originally slated to enter production as a low-build vehicle for private owners to drive in races. It never made it.

Four versions of the car were built—two coupes and two Spiders; all were fitted with a modified version of the Alfa Romeo 1900 2 liter engine delivering 138 horsepower. Top speed of the 2070 pound vehicle (coupe) was 130 mph.

The Spider had low wraparound windows and headlights that were a bit more pointed and less aerodynamic than the coupe's. The two-seat Alfa Romeo featured a multi-tube chassis construction with a light alloy body. Brakes were of light alloy drum with spiral cooling fins. The rear area of the Sportiva influenced the design of the Alfa Romeo 1300 Giulietta Sprint.

FERRARI 410 SA SUPERFAST

The Superfast bore a faint resemblance to the 1956 Alfa Romeo Superflow—mainly in the rear fins. The resemblance stops there. In the true sense, it was simply a one-off model: an old Ferrari chassis with a new body—but a good-looking body nonetheless. Considered significant or at least noteworthy on this model was the two-tone paint scheme with a separation at the hip line, giving the impression that the body was made of two horizontally split halves. This color use became more common on later Ferraris. Other noteworthy features were a double bumper guard, a wide-grooved hood air scoop, very thin door handles, and a curved windshield that gave the impression of no A-pillar. Power came from a 5 liter 340 horsepower 12 cylinder engine. Three other 410SA Superfasts were built by Pininfarina, one in 1960 and two in 1962.

FIAT MULTIPLA MARINE

As the name suggests, the Multipla Marine was designed for the boating set to be utilized as either a vehicle secured on yachts for inland excursion or parked at the beach house for trips to the waterfront and back. Making the vehicle attractive for water sport use, the open-top multiple seater had a wraparound rear bench seat constructed of wooden slats. The front seats were padded. Built over the Fiat 600 cc engine, the Pininfarina-bodied Multipla Marine was one of many leisure vehicles to come out of the Italian coachbuilding fraternity during the 1950s.

RENAULT ETOILE FILANTE

The Renault Etoile Filante or "Shooting Star" was one of the many turbine-powered experimental vehicles of its day. (Other prominent turbine designs arose from the test tracks at Rover, Fiat, Chrysler, and General Motors.) A gas generator in the Shooting Star ran at 35,000 rpm, driving a free-power turbine that developed 270 horsepower. The Shooting Star chassis was of welded tubular construction covered in a plastic skin contributing to the slight vehicle weight of 2090 pounds. Large disc brakes were provided due to the lack of engine braking.

On September 5, 1956 at the Bonneville Salt Flats in Utah, the Shooting Star piloted by Jean Herbert broke the world record for turbine cars by achieving a speed of 195 mph. The body of the Shooting Star was designed by Eiffel Laboratories—named for the man who built the tower.

The advantages of a turbine engine were many—they were light and small with good power output, they required fewer moving parts than a gas engine, no cooling system was required, and a turbine could run on a variety of fuels. But high cost made the turbine quite uneconomical to produce.

ABARTH RECORD

Presented at the 1957 Turin show, the Abarth Record was built solely from stock Fiat parts with a Fiat 600 engine modified by Abarth—thus the Abarth name. The single-seat Abarth Record had four speeds, no reverse, and brakes were fitted on the front wheels only. The body was designed by Scaglione. An initial problem of supplying cool air to the engine without increasing wind drag was solved by slicing a slot in the rear fin. All mechanicals were on the right side of the vehicle to counteract the centrifugal force of track running in a clockwise direction. A line of experimental Bertone Abarths went on to set long distance records in the 500, 750, and 1100 cc categories. The 750, which was built in forty days, ran 6214 miles in three days, averaging 87.4 mph and 40 mpg.

Numerous Abarth Record vehicles with bodies by Pininfarina went on to set distance records for many years after the Bertone models.

CARROZZERIA BERTONE

ALFA ROMEO & FIAT ABARTH RECORD

True experimental bodies, the Alfa Romeo Abarth 1100 and the Fiat Abarth 750 were single seaters built with steel tube structure covered in 0.7 mm aluminum with the sole purpose of setting long-distance driving records. Hence the suffix "Record."

The Fiat Abarth set a record seventy-two-hour driving record of 1181 miles at 102 mph. The engine was mounted just ahead of the rear axle and brakes were placed on the front wheels only. In the same year Pininfarina built the Alfa Romeo Abarth 1100 Record—identical in body style save a slight rear fin alteration—and it went on to set a record for 500 km (310 miles), averaging 122 mph.

Pininfarina went on to body record-breaking Abarths well into the 1960s. Bertone also bodied an Abarth Record in 1957.

FIAT 500 JOLLY

The Fiat 500 Jolly may be one of the most appropriately named experimental vehicles ever. After all, this one was pure fun. The beach car or vacation car was a hot topic for Italian designers during the 1950s (Pininfarina would later produce the Teenager), and the Jolly certainly qualified as a leisure vehicle. Built to hold four passengers, or two passengers and a load of beach-appropriate equipment (or one passenger and even more beach equipment), the Jolly emphasized the outdoor look with basketwork seats and a door that consisted of a narrow cloth strap. The chromium side rails also served as body reinforcements. The screen and steering wheel were detachable.

The compact size and light weight made the Jolly a great choice as the inland vehicle on private yachts.

GHIA IXG

The Ghia IXG was built with the intention of breaking records—speed records. And in building such a vehicle, the area that receives the greatest attention is aerodynamics. With the IXG, the airflow pattern on the top of the car was kept as close as possible to neutral to minimize drag and lift. The driver sat behind the rear wheels to increase road adhesion.

A one-fifth scale model was used in wind-tunnel testing to discover the area of largest positive and negative drag. In these spots designers placed an air inlet and air outlet, respectively. A sharp crease around the car was used to break cross winds. The driver sat inclined to minimize car height. The steering wheel was designed at such an angle to the shaft that it would swing out of the way of the eyes of the driver when turning.

Power was supplied by an 850 cc engine. The vehicle appeared tremendously long but was only 192 inches in length. Long but not that long.

GHIA SELENE

One of the most unusual designs brought out in 1960 (which end is front?) was the Ghia-designed Selene. Conceived in part through the analysis of aircraft design, the Selene took a very futuristic approach to the needs of motorists. The design forecasted the existence of enormous motorways with electronic drive controls and the need to ease the tension of the driver. (They certainly forecasted the latter need correctly.)

Constructing driver's controls that could move in front of either front passenger was a major feature of the driving-ease approach. All controls were grouped on the center console and pedals were mounted on the floor in line with each front seat. Four additional passengers could be accommodated in the rear area with two sets of seats facing each other. A bar and television set were available for the rear passengers.

The engine compartment—the Selene actually didn't have an engine, it was a static prototype—was placed in the rear, far from the occupants. This was another design similarity to the contemporary aircraft layout: engines rearward and driver far forward.

PININFARINA 'X'

Created around a Fiat engine, the Pininfarina 'X' had a completely different body shape resulting from the rhomboidal layout of the four wheels—that is, one center front, one on each side behind the rear doors, and one center rear. The single rear wheel propelled the vehicle while the front wheel steered.

In keeping with the rounded, egg-like look, three plastic-covered headlights were placed directly over three bumper guards. The vehicle appeared very unbalanced when viewed from the front.

The overall purpose was to create a vehicle capable of higher speeds and lower fuel consumption through aerodynamics. Its drag coefficient was 0.2, much less than contemporary models. A Fiat 1100 engine was mounted over the right rear wheel; a luggage compartment was over the left. The egg-shaped design was one that Battista "Pinin" Farina, the founder of Pininfarina, thought was the optimum automobile form. Although most current vehicles incorporate rounded body lines, few have taken the look to the extreme envisioned with the 'X.'

A PFY was also developed a year later with similar styling but with a conventional placement of the four wheels.

GHIA KART

The Ghia Kart would never be mistaken for a luxury-class sedan; after all, where would the television sit?

This study of pure line was undertaken in order to show the great possibilities that any vehicle, even the simplest, can reach through an accurate survey of style and the work of qualified designers. (At least that's what the press material stated.)

The light body could be completely disassembled thanks to the use of rapid aircraft clips. The Kart was intended for the connoisseur, for small contests or private use.

The Kart had a wheelbase of 44 inches, height of 27 inches, and overall length of only 82 inches.

1 9 6 1

GHIA SELENE II

Ghia designers furthered the concepts of the Selene I introduced a year earlier by creating the easier-to-look-at Selene II. The Selene II design emphasized aerodynamics, with smooth lines and a round style and roadholding with the addition of a tail pin. A short wheelbase (88 inches compared to a 191 inch overall vehicle length) gave exceptional stability while cornering.

The extreme-front driving position and vast glass area gave the driver exceptional visibility. The interior featured three seats: a center-front driver's seat and two passenger seats facing rearward to lower the roof height. A lift-up canopy allowed entrance for the driver, while two side doors were available for the passengers. The rear compartment featured a television to keep the passengers occupied. The mid-mounted engine position could accommodate powerplants from 1000 cc to 2500 cc.

ROVER T4

The "T" in the Rover T4 stood for a much researched engine option of this period: turbine power. Turbine-powered vehicles appeared from the research departments of Renault, Fiat, Chrysler, and General Motors during the 1950s and 1960s. None went into production. The first Rover turbine, the Jet 1, was built in 1950. It was followed by the T2 sedan, the T3 coupe with four-wheel drive and rear-mounted engine, and the T4 front-wheel drive which closely resembled the piston-engined production Rover 2000. (In fact, the two vehicles shared many body panels.) The T4 came the closest to production of the four turbines with its 2S/140 gas-turbine motor front-mounted and driving the front wheels. The front-wheel drive allowed the transmission shaft tunnel to be used as a conduit for hot engine air. Rear suspension was independent. Performance was impressive with a top speed of 115 mph but fuel economy (the bane of all turbines) was between 16 and 20 mpg. In 1963 a Rover-BRM turbine raced at LeMans.

ALFA ROMEO 2600 SZ

The 2600 SZ (Spring Zagato), based on the largest range in the Alfa Romeo stable, was characterized by its unusually large Alfa Romeo grille. The square headlights, a somewhat uncommon sight during this period, sat behind a glass cover. A 2+2, the 2600 SZ was powered by a 6 cylinder 2583 cc engine that generated 165 horsepower with 3 carburetors. The aluminum-bodied coupe had a top speed of 130 mph.

BERTONE TESTUDO

Built over a shortened Corvair Monza Coupe chassis, the Testudo stood only 3 feet 6 inches high. Much like the earlier BAT Bertone experimentals, the Testudo was a study in aerodynamics. Aside from typical aerodynamic thoughts like a low nose and retractable headlights which popped up like bug eyes, the car's extreme side line displayed Bertone's interest in side aerodynamics.

A couple of intriguing features of the Testudo were the rectangular steel steering wheel (which never caught on) and a door, window, and windscreen that were hinged to raise together. The side body sills had to be stepped over to enter the vehicle. The roof was all glass and the rounded front windshield blended into the side windows due to the lack of an A-pillar. Some interior features were a grab rail mounted on the passenger's dashboard, contoured seats, and an extremely thin instrument panel. The engine was placed in the tail—notice the lack of a front radiator grille—with air intake vents positioned just behind the side windows. The body lines of the Testudo influenced the design of the Porsche 924, Porsche 928, and Mazda RX-7.

PININFARINA PF SIGMA

The PF Sigma design was based on an idea from Gianni Mazzocchi, editor of the magazine *Quattroroute* calling for fourteen technical safety solutions. The implemented solutions found on the Sigma were: 1) The center of the vehicle was quite inflexible and the front and rear have accident crumple zones to absorb energy—a major area of research at auto R & D facilities currently. 2) Special front and rear panels were designed to prevent mechanical parts from entering the passenger compartment upon collision. 3) A larger and padded steering wheel and steering rod was designed not to penetrate the passenger compartment. 4) Sliding doors were added which were considered safer in a collision. 5) Rounded, partial rubber bumpers and external surfaces were used to prevent injuries to pedestrians. 6) Internal upholstery was designed to protect occupants in case of collision. 7) The construction of a well padded dashboard. 8) The windscreen ejected outward in a collision. 9) A windshield protection shield eliminated driver and passenger contact with the car interior. 10) Embedded windshield wipers improved driver visibility. 11) A headrest and ergonomical seats provided occupant safety and comfort. 12) A well distributed ventilation system meant maximum comfort. 13) A white exterior color for better visibility during day and night. 14) Safety belts for all four seats.

ALFA ROMEO GIULIA 1600 CANGURO

This styling exercise by Bertone was so low to the ground that the bottom of the seats determined ground clearance. The bucket seats sat in a channel below the belly pan giving the expression "driving by the seat of your pants" a whole new meaning. The anatomical seats were perforated and the bottoms and backs were covered with loose-fitting fabric allowing the occupant's body to breathe. Also unique to the Canguro, which incidentally translates to kangaroo, was the method of bonding the windscreens to the pillars à la the aircraft industry rather than using the typical rubber seal. The curved waist line of the Canguro (the area where the glass and body meet) was intriguing because it created very strange window shapes. The doors of the Canguro were curved into the roof giving the occupants easier access to the seats. A new treatment of ventilation was found in the form of a vent in the shape of a four-leaf clover on the side pillar. The vehicle was only 42 inches high and the only hinged glass was small sections on each side window. Some bad news for collectors: The car was destroyed in 1970 with some parts sold off.

A similar car produced by the Italian coachbuilder Zagato called the TZ2 was built and raced in 1965.

FIAT ABARTH 1000 SPIDER

The Fiat Abarth 1000 was a low-slung, rear-engine Spider with a wraparound windshield. The doors were small, taking up only slightly more than half of the body's height. The four round quartz-iodine headlamps were placed behind a clear aerodynamic shield. The body was all aluminum, weighing only 1400 pounds. Power came from an Abarth 1000 engine on a Fiat 850 coupe chassis.

The interior contained individually padded headrests and the steering wheel swiveled to create easier entrance and exit.

The tail of the Abarth 1000 was at the same height as the headrests to try to eliminate excess cockpit wind.

FIAT ABARTH 1000

Simply a styling exercise on the Fiat Abarth 850 Chassis—as was the 1964 Fiat Abarth 1000—this Pininfarina version had many of the same lines as the 1964 Spider version designed by Pininfarina. A significant difference from the coupe was the ability of the entire roof and windows—front and side—to tilt forward to a nearly vertical position. The doors, as with the Spider version, were extremely small and opened out. Slots under the rear window aided in ventilation, and power came from a 74 horsepower engine. The headlights were placed under acetate, like many Pininfarina models of that period.

The interior of the Fiat Abarth 1000 was modest with only two circular gauges set behind the steering wheel. The body of the coupe was all aluminum.

ALFA ROMEO OSI SCARABEO

The 2-seat Scarabeo, bodied by the coachbuilder OSI, was one of many design experiments of the 1960s to emphasize a long, pointed nose with highly curved front wheel arches. What differentiated the Scarabeo from many other designs was the chopped-off treatment of the rear end. A descendant of experiments with weight distribution and engine placement, the 4 cylinder DOHC Giulia 1600 engine was mounted transversely immediately behind the passenger seat. The tubular chassis was utilized as a fuel tank. The rear wheel arches appeared as shoulders with a huge air inlet serving the rear-mounted engine. The body was made of fiberglass. Three versions of the Scar-

abeo were built: two coupes and one Spider. The first version (pictured here) was characterized by the four headlights and an abruptly terminated rear end. The later coupe and Spider displayed a longer, less chopped-off rear area.

Interior amenities on the first coupe were scarce, with two round gauges positioned over the simply styled steering wheel. Entrance to the vehicle was facilitated by the raising of a single-piece cockpit cover hinged at the windshield base. Its overall appearance gave the impression that the vehicle was ready for the race circuit rather than the roadway.

GHIA VANESSA

The Ghia-designed Vanessa or "Butterfly" was purely a niche vehicle. That niche: the car for the woman.

Built on a Fiat 850 chassis, the Vanessa was a four-seat, two-door coupe only 50 inches high. Front seats had adjustable backrests and the driver's seat could swivel. The rear seat folded to form a loading surface easily accessible through the wide-top hinged rear door. A portion of the rear seat folded down to form a baby seat. A folded pushcart with baby seat stored in the front.

The luggage compartment had a spring-loaded hood and the interior contained several compartments "each designed for a specific purpose." Those purposes were not made clear in the Ghia press material.

All instruments consisted of warning lights, grouped in a single dial. The speedometer was equipped with an audio signal to warn the driver when speeds of 50 or 100 km (31 or 62 mph) were exceeded.

The car also featured electrically operated windows, rear window defroster, removable transparent panel to create a sun roof, a fire extinguisher and, maybe to keep the vehicle from becoming too feminine, a cigar lighter with warning bell.

VAUXHALL XVR

Designed to provide outstanding handling and a high degree of driver and passenger safety, the XVR had a wide track (56 inches), low center of gravity, good weight distribution, and fully independent suspension—a feature that has become commonplace on today's production vehicles.

The doors of the vehicle pivoted upward and outward on a single central windshield strut. This provided excellent side vision but also created a blind spot directly in front of the driver. The door handles were flush with the body surface. The entire hood assembly pivoted forward for access to the engine and spare wheel. The vertically sliding rear window was electrically controlled and air ducts by the occupants' feet permitted a controlled flow of warm or cool air through the passenger compartment. An electrically controlled mechanism retracted the headlamps into the body.

1967

FERRARI DINO

The design of the 1960 Ferrari Dino by Pininfarina was significant because it was a forerunner to many of the mass-produced Ferraris of the eighties. This two seater had gull-wing doors, collapsible steering wheel, adjustable front and rear stabilizers, and big air intakes on each side. The front wing could be adjusted for downward thrust only when the vehicle was at rest, but adjustment to the rear wing could occur while the car moved. A single windshield wiper served the vast windshield.

The interior was well padded and special research went into the design of energy absorption areas. A small row of round gauges lined an area of the dashboard to the left of the driver—the vehicle was right-hand drive—while the speedometer was larger and set directly behind the steering wheel, hinting that the vehicle was for driving at notable speeds.

The car also was notable in a Hollywood manner with its appearance in the movie "A Clockwork Orange."

1967

LAMBORGHINI MARZAL

This Bertone design offered a huge amount of glass area (48.4 square feet including an all-glass roof) and gull-winged doors that hinged at the roofline and provided easy access to the front and rear seats. The doors were almost completely glass allowing outside viewers a clear shot of the interior. The rear window was composed of hexagonal panels that formed a honeycomb-type configuration. The honeycomb theme was extended to the interior with hexagonal-shaped instrument gauges. The interior color followed the metallic look of the exterior with four silver seats separated by a central tunnel.

At the front, a rubber bumper protected the six iodine headlights. The Marzal was powered by a 175 horsepower in-line 6 cylinder engine, which was actually a split Lamborghini V12, 4 OHC engine mounted above the rear axle. To create space for four seats, the engine was set transversely and the engine and transmission shifted rearward. A small luggage compartment in the vehicle's front provided limited cargo capacity.

After its debut at the 1967 Geneva Motor Show, the Marzal appeared at the Monaco Grand Prix where it completed the opening lap piloted by Prince Rainier.

O.S.I. SILVER FOX

The O.S.I. Silver Fox certainly added a fresh look to aerodynamic styling. Rather than attempt to improve sleekness the old-fashioned way, the Silver Fox stepped in (actually, wheeled in) another direction with what could be labelled the "twin-pontoon" design. Power for the vehicle originated from an Alpine 1000 placed in the left pontoon behind the passenger. The driver sat in the right pontoon. An air brake controlled from the driver's seat helped slow the vehicle after it cut through the wind, and adjustable spoilers on two levels could alter both vehicle drag and lift. Coefficient of drag was 0.26. Although visibly separate, the two occupants could converse via a common open section joining the two tubes. Gull-wing doors were almost necessary on a vehicle that threw conventional styling out the window.

ALFA ROMEO P33

Pininfarina's Alfa Romeo P33 was one of the first wedge-shape vehicles by the Italian coachbuilder. In theory, by using the wedge design, the entire car body would exert force on the wheels by utilizing the passing slip screen, thus increasing roadholding. This mid-engined, two seater built on a Fiat Tipo 33 chassis had a raked roll bar with adjustable aileron. The front of the wedge terminated with a row of small quartz-iodine headlights—six—and a thin rubber bumper. The two small doors opened up, not out, and against the wind.

Some safety features included in the P33 were an automatic fire extinguisher built into the car and a seat belt apparatus designed to reduce deceleration strain in an impact.

BERTONE CARABO

The Bertone Carabo is considered a significant vehicle not merely for its striking shape (the Carabo is typically referred to as the father of the "one-box" shape as well as the main influence on the design of the Lamborghini Countach; the celebrated Marcello Gandini penned both designs while with Bertone), but also for what may not be initially suspected looking at its wild shape: safety.

The safety scheme centered in two areas: color and glass. The use of black, green, and orange created a visible vehicle, one that would immediately catch the attention of other drivers. The glass was made of a new type of material. Developed by a Belgian company, the new safety glass consisted of two thin layers of highly resistant material with a plastic sheet compressed between. The copper-tinted glass was half the weight of normal safety glass. The glass also prevented those outside from seeing in; whether this is viewed as a safety feature is dependent on one's definition of "safety."

Powering the 49 inch–high Carabo was a 230 horsepower Alfa Romeo engine that claimed a top speed of 160 mph. Also designed into the Carabo were a reclining driving position and an instrument panel that lit when a button was pressed.

The final vehicle was completed in only ten weeks from the day Bertone took delivery of the chassis. And in case you're wondering, the Carabo name comes from the scissor-type opening of the doors—beetle-like, or Carabo, in Italian.

DE TOMASO MANGUSTA SPYDER

The Mangusta Spyder was the only alteration in the Mangusta body style ever produced by Ghia. A true one-off, the Spyder was based on the standard Mangusta two door, two seater with a V8 powerplant. The styling changes completed by Ghia's Giorgetto Giugiaro were the design of a new rear deck cover to include a couple of rows of louvers and the attachment of the stainless steel door-window frames to the body rather than the doors. The interior was very similar to the Mangusta coupe with Ghia saying, "It is characterized by maximum comfort and maximum functionality." Window mechanisms were electrically operated.

Although a top was never officially available on the Spyder, the initial owner of the vehicle constructed one. With or without the roof cover, speed topped out at about 150 mph.

FERRARI 250 P5

Pininfarina took the design of the 1967 Dino a bit further with the Ferrari 250 P5. The vehicle might have been a bit more radical but a hint of eighties Ferrari can be spotted on this model with the carved body-side air intakes. A pure-styling attention-getter, the 250 P5 looked powerful from any angle. But it's clear that the designers de-emphasized crash-worthiness with nary a bumper.

The rear of the vehicle consisted of a transparent compartment housing a V-12 Ferrari powerplant along with a securely strapped-in spare tire. Gull-wing doors, eight headlights and lots of glass were also characteristics of the Ferrari 250 P5.

GIUGIARO MANTA BIZZARRINI

A major difference between the Manta Bizzarrini and other car designs of the day was the length of the nose—or rather the lack of length. Rather than a long sharp nose, typical of designs of this period, the Manta displayed a stub nose with a short overhang. This indicated, or rather, necessitated, the rear/mid-placement of the LeMans Chevy V8 engine. This also translated to minimal luggage space.

The front windshield slant of 15 degrees and the low seating position typically translated into poor visibility. This was reduced in the Manta with the use of three horizontal wings on the vehicle's hood which could be viewed through and adjusted from the interior. The wings folded shut at high speeds.

The interior featured three separate seats arranged in a straight line. The driver sat in the center. The high rear end compromised rear sight, so a horizontal opening was added to the rear window above the tail.

The three-seat coupe (that's not said often) appeared very tightly designed with a single line flowing from the front to rear. The vehicle is also significant in that it was the first independent design from Giorgetto Giugiaro of Bertone and Ghia fame.

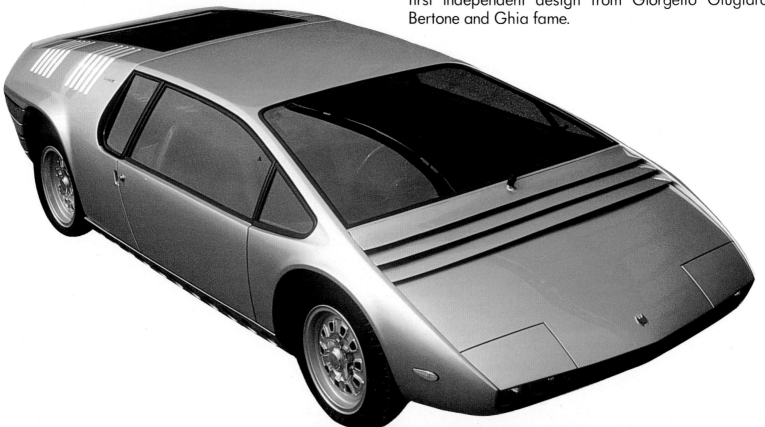

ITALDESIGN IGUANA

The Iguana—along with three other contemporary concept cars, the Pininfarina P33 and Bertone Carabo—was based on the Alfa Romeo 33/2 chassis. The two-seat Iguana was characterized by the deep front hood vent that created two mud guard-type humps over the front wheels. The vast use of glass—large windshield, clear roof—provided good visibility. The rear engine was also visible through the glassed rear deck.

The rear end proposed an innovative solution to deal with negative lift using a broad stabilizer which was ad-justed electrically, and in addition, could be positioned so as to aid maneuvers when reversing.

Sparsity characterized the Iguana's interior with an instrument panel that overhung the dashboard and included only relevant switches on a vertical panel between the two seats.

The car became somewhat awkward-looking when the headlights rose. In combination with the Alfa Romeo crest and slotted air intakes, the headlights formed the eyes of a thin-lipped, smirking expression.

1969

AUTOBIANCHI RUNABOUT

If this car looks familiar, it's because it formed a basis for the successful 1972 Fiat X 1/9. Designed by Gandini of Bertone and based on the Autobianchi A112 chassis, this mid-engined (the engine had to be moved from the A112's front engine placement), rear-drive two seater had a wild, striped two-color interior. The lights were mounted on the forward-raked roll bar, giving new meaning to the term "high beams." Although many critics of the period called the Runabout a crazy car, Mr. Bertone readily admitted that the Runabout was conceived as purely a fun car. How fun? The sole instrument was a compass.

50

BMW 2800 SPICUP

This Bertone design took the BMW 2800 chassis and styled a two-seat coupe around it. The Spicup featured an electrically retractable two-piece roof that slid into the roll bar. The Spicup had one feature that is still very uncommon on BMWs: pop-up headlights. The side emblem motif resembled that of the classic BMW 507. The vehicle's instrumentation was very typical with analog gauges set behind the steering wheel, but the seats were of a two-tone variety with a semicircular padded section on the bottom that conjured up an image that the designer hadn't considered: it looked like a toilet seat. This one-off (the car, not the seat) was eventually sold to a private customer.

FERRARI 512S

The low slender front end of the Pininfarina Ferrari 512S was quite similar to the production 512S. Powered by a 4.9 liter V12, the 512S had a very low profile at only 39 inches, but its stance was considerable with a body width of 77 inches. The tubular chassis with riveted light alloy panels provided body rigidity. The exposed rear end allowed for increased ventilation to the engine, brakes, transmission, etc.

Setting the car apart from some of its predecessors (and contemporaries), particularly the 1960 Abarth 2000, the 512S utilized less glass area, with the engine covered with black louvers rather than glass. The right-hand rather than left-hand drive of the 512S was due to the fact that the actual racing 512S chassis was used; it was right-hand drive. An interesting note about the 512S was its slight English slant. Surely, the sloping, aerodynamic exterior design was classic Italian. But inside, red-and-black-checked seat upholstery created an Italian/British hybrid.

FIAT ABARTH 2000

The Pininfarina-designed Fiat Abarth 2000 was intended to explore experimental queries on a racing level in terms of aerodynamics and engine ventilation. But the vehicle was more publicity than an indication of future production plans. Power originated from a rear-mounted 2000 cc engine.

A row of quartz-iodine headlights was integrated into the front hood above two air intakes. A built-in fire extinguisher could be controlled automatically or manually. The body was reinforced with fiberglass cloth between tubular sections.

The huge rear exhaust gave the appearance that the vehicle was jet powered. Pretty close: top speed was 170 mph.

FIAT TEENAGER

Designed by Pininfarina in 1969, the Fiat 128 Teenager would be at home today in a California beachfront driveway. Built on a shortened floor pan of the Fiat 128, this leisure vehicle could seat seven—with little room for beach balls or lunch basket—and had a fold-down windshield à la Chrysler Jeeps. A special locking storage area beneath the rear seats held a pair of walkie-talkies. With no doors or roof, the Teenager was not appropriate transportation for inclement weather. Power for the youth-orientated weekender came from a small 4 cylinder engine generating 55 horsepower.

MERCEDES-BENZ C111-I

The Mercedes-Benz C111-I was the first of a series of true experiments on wheels with "C" designations. The C111-I was born out of the desire at Mercedes to produce a new sports car. The C111-I was therefore a rolling experiment, testing ideas for future vehicles. Mercedes' emphasis was to build a vehicle that was not just fast but that could be mass-produced. Designing a driveable, comfortable, and quiet-running vehicle was also an important consideration. A total of six C111-I were built.

The gull-winged C111-I utilized a mid-car Wankel rotary engine—the first such engine placement in a Mercedes in eighty years. It was also the first Mercedes to use fiberglass. The front suspension was eventually used in the S-Class Series sedans. Top speed was 170 mph with a 0 to 62 mph time of 5 seconds. The C111-I's style was a departure from the traditional Mercedes. But it was a fine departure. The Mercedes star looked every bit as comfortable on the sloping hood of the C111-I as it did on any other vehicle.

PORSCHE 911 4-SEATER

The Porsche 911 4-seater was one of a few Porsche cars styled by Italian coachbuilder Pininfarina. The "family" 911 was built on a wheelbase of 97 inches, 7.5 inches longer than a standard 911. The 2.2 liter 6 cylinder engine and transmission remained unchanged. Weight of the vehicle exceeded 2500 pounds and weight distribution was an unacceptable 39 percent front, 61 percent rear. These factors, along with a turning circle of 38 feet, doomed the vehicle to the realm of pure experiment.

In 1975 the car was modified with a Carrera look: front spoiler and wider wings. A 210 horsepower Carrera 2.7 liter engine was also installed.

To this day, rumors of a four-seat and four-door Porsche linger. The projected date of the debut (according to those who like to guess at these things—usually journalists) has fluctuated from 1995 to 1997. The name typically cited: the 989.

SIGMA GRAND PRIX

The Sigma Grand Prix experimental racer by Pininfarina was a Formula 1 design project built of light alloy. Conceived by the Swiss magazine *Revue Automobile* along with Pininfarina and other specialists, the Sigma Grand Prix featured a shockproof bearing structure with differential resistance; a ring bumper to avoid locking between cars with uncovered wheels; mud-guard flaps to prevent stone flying; a fuel tank designed by Pirelli and Pininfarina that achieved excellent stress resistance, heat insulation and puncturing resistance; automatic fire prevention plant to protect the passenger compartment and the engine bay; seven-branch safety belt; protection against oil leaks; fluorescent colored area for better visibility; and stabilizers with variable and negative lift.

BMW 2200ti GARMISCH

The 2200ti Garmisch was a proposal from Bertone for a future BMW. Although never put into production, the Garmisch was not too far from production lines, and it has been said that it inspired the BMW 520 and 525 series.

Some distinctive features on the Garmisch were the covered headlights and a somewhat altered, twin-hexagonal signature BMW kidney grille set above a rather large mouth-like air intake. That shape was continued on the rear window where a hexagon pattern similar to the 1967 Bertone Marzal appeared. Interesting too was the body-side groove running from front to rear. This design feature was found also on many Pininfarina designs of the same period. The car also lacked side-view mirrors. The Garmisch was never sold and is now the property of BMW AG.

ITALDESIGN TAPIRO

The wedge-shaped Tapiro was based on the mechanicals of the Volkswagen/Porsche 914/16. This highly glassed vehicle had gull-wing doors connected to a backbone running the length of the car from the windshield to the truncated rear. The backbone was also the center piece for an air intake above the windshield.

The most distinguishing feature of the vehicle's front view was the central depression in the hood created by the rising crest on the mud guards. The angle of the front windshield was nearly the same as the sharp sloping nose. The glass encompassing the rear of the Tapiro was rounded to provide better aerodynamics at high speeds.

The car's instrumentation was reduced to a minimum with a compact grouping of gauges centered behind the steering wheel. The forward-flipping hood revealed a 2.4 liter engine that output 220 horsepower. Small baggage space was available over the engine and transmission.

LANCIA STRATOS

Don't try to find the doors—there weren't any, at least not the conventional type. To enter the Stratos, the windshield lifted up, like a mouth opening, allowing the driver to step into the vehicle. The steering column folded away automatically when the "door" opened. Very distinctive, to say the least.

The Bertone-designed Stratos was built over Lancia Fulvia 1.6 HF mechanicals with a mid-engine layout. The mid-car positioning of the engine allowed the designers to push the driver's seating to the extreme front giving the driver excellent visibility over the short, slanting nose. Ten rectangular lights lined the vehicle's front.

The events following the introduction of the show car Stratos were a bit atypical. One year after its introduction a less extreme prototype was produced with a Ferrari 246 V6 engine. Three years later, in 1974, a production version was built to homologate the vehicle for Group 4 Special GT Cars category (rally racing). A minimum of 500 vehicles had to be produced for the vehicle to qualify for rally racing, although rumors are that only about 250 actually found owners due in major part to the fuel crisis. The rally car found great success between 1974 and 1976.

MERCEDES-BENZ C111-II

The Mercedes-Benz C111-II was introduced in March 1970, five months after the first experimental "C", the C111-I. The C111-II was a revised version of its namesake with a four-rotor engine rather than the three of its predecessor. The new rotary engine developed 350 horsepower propelling the vehicle from 0–62 mph in 4.8 seconds. Top speed was 187 mph. The C11-II had other modifications such as improved rear and side vision with the side windows extended rearward and the waist line lowered. The retractable headlights were electrically operated rather than foot-operated as in the C111-I. The luggage area was even increased with the redesign of the exhaust system. With all the changes, the C111-II weighed in 65 pounds heavier than the first experimental "C".

The vehicle generated such a huge response, Mercedes seriously considered small-series production. Doubts regarding the reliability of the Wankel engine and the energy crisis crushed those plans.

PININFARINA MODULO

The Modulo prototype was an extraordinarily progressive design (remember, this was 1970) built on a Ferrari 512S floor pan and constructed of two shells joined at the waist line. To access the passenger compartment, the entire canopy, including the front and side windows, slid forward over the front hood. The vehicle was only three feet high. Inside, two spherical controls—resembling bowling balls—housed the controls for fresh air vents and other cabin controls. Power came from a 550 horsepower V12. In 1971,

the Modulo, a design penned by Paulo Martin, received the Styling Award from *Automobile Quarterly*. It is routinely referred to nowadays as one of the most significant automobile designs of the 1970s.

In theory, the Modulo could be changed in form by simply eliminating some body panels—sedan to coupe and coupe to convertible.

According to Pininfarina, the Modulo was an expression of culture.

VOLVO EXPERIMENTAL SAFETY VEHICLES

During the 1970s, Volvo produced a fleet of experimental safety vehicles whose only purpose was to die a punishing death for the sake of passenger safety research. The research was meant to evaluate many different solutions to the safety question. Features included on various versions of the Volvo cars were: semi-passive safety belts which came into operation when the car was started; air bags on the rear window shelf to protect back seat passengers in a rear-end collision; protruding bumpers; a spring-loaded steering wheel which automatically pulled the wheel six inches forward—and away from the driver—when a decelerator sensor was activated during a collision; circular-sweep headlight wipers (which looked like tiny propellers); reinforced body structure; an engine-mounting system that forced the engine under the vehicle in a frontal crash; padded front seat backrests; and a nascent anti-lock braking system.

ALFA ROMEO ALFASUD CAIMANO

The uniqueness of the Italdesign-penned Alfasud Caimano lay in the use of a front engine rather than the mid-engine placement of most European concept cars of the day. Therefore, instead of having a cab forward feel, the vehicle, with its long nose, offered a cab backward appearance.

The windshield and door hinged at the windshield base and flipped forward in a complete unit. At the top of the trapezium-shaped rear pillars sat a spoiler that could be adjusted according to vehicle lift requirements.

Inside the Caimano was a tubular-shaped instrument display for the tachometer, and the fuel, water temperature, and oil gauges.

Probably the most convenient feature, given the glass roof and door unit, was a small window on each side of the vehicle placed at passenger body height allowing an occupant to pay a toll or gas attendant (or get some fresh air) without flipping up the entire roof. Also interesting were the horizontal wheel cover vents.

ALFA ROMEO 33 SPIDER

The Alfa Romeo 33 Spider designed by Pininfarina was very similar to the 1968 Alfa Romeo P33 in its wedge shape; the 1971 version had an even more pronounced, extreme wedge profile, interrupted only by the front wheel well bumps.

The mid-engined V8 vehicle had a very small windscreen, a thin roll bar and narrow front with elliptical headlights housed within wraparound rubber. Air entered the vehicle through an opening at either side of the lights and also through deep cuts located on the surface of the vehicle just behind the passenger compartment and before the rear wheels, rather than on the vehicle's side.

The interior was rather sparse with a small row of five gauges to the driver's right and a large speedometer placed directly behind the steering wheel.

ITALDESIGN MASERATI BOOMERANG

As with many designs of the day, the Italdesign-conceived Maserati Boomerang had ample glass area and a very low profile—the windshield angle was a sharp 13 degrees (this compares to the already sharp angle of the Italdesign [Giugiaro] Manta). An angle any sharper would greatly impede visibility—or make it simply non-existent. The doors comprised mostly a glass window which was split into two halves; the upper half was fixed, while the lower half could be tilted.

Furthering its study of driver convenience and safety, Italdesign clustered all instrumentation inside the circular steering wheel. The speedometer was set in the middle with other gauges forming a half-circle above and switches for various controls below. The steering column was split and movements were transmitted via a chain drive. The arrangement of controls and split steering column provided greater visibility and safety in a collision. Power came from the Maserati Bora 4.7 liter V8 mounted behind the passenger compartment.

The name Boomerang arises from the contention that the design concepts presented in the car would return in future vehicles.

MERCEDES-BENZ EXPERIMENTAL SAFETY VEHICLES

ESF 03

From 1971 through 1974, Mercedes-Benz developed five vehicles with the expressed interest of safety. Dubbed ESF 03, 05, 13, 22, and 24, the vehicles featured amenities such as a passive safety belt system (the motorized kind that have become so common today), an air bag, sturdy seats with integrated headrests, shoulder supports for side impacts, a recessed instrument panel, hydraulic shock absorbers, side impact protection, and operating controls marked by easy-to-read symbols.

All vehicles were crash-tested frontal, side, and rear. The most important requirement was protection of the occupant during a front crash into a fixed barrier at 50 mph. ESF 03, 13, and 22 were even drop-tested from 0.5 meters.

The features tested in the ESF program led to safer, stronger vehicles worldwide, with the results of these tests shared with other manufacturers in an internationally sponsored conference on experimental safety vehicles.

ESF 05

ESF 13

ESF 22

ESF 24

ESF 03
Presented on May 26, 1971
Specifications :
Frontal impact against fixed barrier **80 km/h**
Side impact against fixed pole 25 km/h

ESF 05
Presented on Oct. 26, 1971
Specifications :
Frontal impact against fixed barrier **80 km/h**
Frontal impact against fixed pole 80 km/h
Side impact against fixed pole 25 km/h
Side impact against fixed barrier 25 km/h
Rear-end impact 80 km/h
Drop test 0.5 m

ESF 13
Presented on May 31, 1972
Specifications :
Frontal impact against fixed barrier **80 km/h**
Frontal impact against fixed pole 80 km/h
Side impact against fixed pole 25 km/h
Side impact against fixed barrier 25 km/h
Rear-end impact 80 km/h
Drop test 0.5 m

ESF 22
Presented on March 13, 1973
Specifications :
Frontal impact against fixed barrier **65 km/h**
Frontal impact against fixed pole 50 km/h
Side impact against fixed pole 20 km/h
Side impact against vehicle 35 km/h
Rear-end impact 50 km/h
Oblique impact with moving barrier 65 km/h
Drop test 0.5 m

ESF 24
Presented on June 3, 1974
Specifications :
Frontal impact against fixed barrier **65 km/h**
All other impact modes
Correspond to Mercedes-Benz
S-Class safety level

NSU RO 80

The NSU RO 80 was a hard-top 2+2 convertible—one that transformed into a convertible not with manual removal of the top, but by an entire roof that rotated and shifted towards the rear of the car and disappeared on top of the trunk. The end result was more like a large sunroof than a pure convertible since all the support pillars remained intact. Developed by Pininfarina, the vehicle also had two rear doors which opened against the wind. Doors of this type were actually against the law, but by installing a device that made it impossible to open the back doors without the front doors already opened, Pininfarina got around the law.

The color combination was, if nothing else, distinct with its two-tone, swooping style. The interior featured very solid comfortable seats and an abundance of round instrument gauges. Power for the vehicle came from a rotary engine.

The NSU RO 80 appeared one year after the radical Pininfarina Modulo. Quite a contrast in styles, which shows the talent that made Pininfarina one of Europe's top coachbuilders.

FRUA PORSCHE 914/16

The coachbuilder Frua in 1971 built this streamlined coupe over the mechanicals of the Porsche 914/16. The car was characterized by the slats along the side extending from the rear pillar to the flat rear end. The air intakes for the mid-mounted engine were small and fore of the rear wheels. The front was somewhat un-Porsche like with its sharp nose and extremely thin front and rear bumpers.

Originally, the Frua Porsche was destined for small series production, but a disagreement between the customer for whom the car was built and the designer—lasting five years—caused the design to stay forever a one of a kind.

BMW TURBO

The BMW Turbo was a two seater, high-performance vehicle emphasizing streamlined styling. The large glass area provided excellent visibility with slats behind the door pillars angled, enhancing rearward vision.

Designed to study the maximum attainable active and passive safety levels, the front and rear body sections were engineered so that in a minor collision the damaged areas reshaped by means of a flameproof foam package. Part of the passive safety equipment was an automatic seat belt system. When the belts were not fastened, the car was immobile. Additional safety-related devices were an anti-skid system and pillars for the gull-wing doors which continued across the roof to form a strong roll-over bar.

The BMW Turbo was powered by a mid-engine 2 liter 4 cylinder fuel-injected power plant cooled by cold air directed through a scoop on the underside of the front panel, then through a tunnel into the engine compartment.

Styling elements from the BMW Turbo found their way onto later BMW vehicles in the form of the M1 and 850i.

1972

CITROEN CAMARGUE

The Camargue designed by Bertone was based on the mechanicals of the Citroën GS. The front-wheel-drive vehicle was circled by an unusual flat surface rather than the complete vertical or rounded door panel of most cars. Also present was typical Bertone heavy-glass treatment. The curved tinted glass—also a common Bertone characteristic—even covered the headlights. Note the pivot points of the windshield wipers, both set on the outside because of the curved glass. Compared to other vehicles from the Bertone stable introduced during the early 70s—like the 1970 Stratos prototype, 1974 Bravo, and even the 1973 Trapeze with its distinctive seat arrangement—the Camargue was rather conservatively styled.

AUDI-NSU TRAPEZE

The key feature of this Bertone design is stated in its name: Trapeze. That is, trapezium shape—not the body, but the seat arrangement. For passenger comfort, the two front seats were very close together, while the rear seats were placed far apart—against the car's side—with the engine housing lying between. This arrangement flew in the face of most mid-engine designs that typically incorporated barely enough rear passenger room for two small dogs. But in the Trapeze the rear occupants could stretch out their legs, thus allowing a four-passenger car within a rather short wheelbase. The rear track measured seven inches wider than the front track because of the interior seat arrangement.

The rounded front windshield, six headlights, and the color—purple inside and out—gave the Trapeze a bit more distinctiveness.

1973

AUTOBIANCHI A 112 GIOVANI

The Autobianchi A 112 Giovani (mouthful, huh?) was designed by Pininfarina with youthful applications in mind; hence, a snug interior. (Giovani means "young" in Italian.) This two seater had a removable hard top converting the vehicle to a targa-type. The two-tone paint work—orange and white—made the vehicle appear to have drastically cut wheel wells when viewed from the side. No high-tech features on this uncomplicated, somewhat boxy design, but nonetheless it still never saw a production line.

The Giovani appeared at a time when Pininfarina began favoring the practical production-type styles, rather than the outrageous, purely stylistic experiments like the 1970 Modulo.

FIAT X1/23 CITY CAR

This two-seat electric vehicle from Fiat certainly had the look of a vehicle with an unusual power source. Consider the extremely short front and rear area. Not much room in either for anything but a small electric engine.

The range of the X1/23 was 45 miles at a constant 31 mph. A top speed of 47 mph could barely get the wind blowing through your hair, but then again, the whole purpose of the City Car and other electric vehicles of its day was to provide economical and environmentally friendly city transportation, not high speed, autobahn-type travel.

Power for the front-wheel-drive vehicle came from a 13.5 horsepower DC motor. Yardney nickel-zinc batteries were used rather than the conventional lead-acid. Curb weight was 1810 pounds, somewhat heavy for a vehicle of this size until the weight of the batteries alone—370 pounds—was considered.

PORSCHE LONG-LIFE CAR

The Porsche Long-Life Car was a research project with the goal of reducing the scrappage rate of vehicles and thus conserving energy and resources by increasing a car's life span—ten years at the time of this project. To achieve this goal, Porsche concentrated on two areas: reduction of wear and tear and selection of materials.

The first area was addressed by using hydrodynamic clutches, contactless ignition systems, and efficient oil and air filtration, among other things.

Selection of materials meant choosing those materials that could be recycled or would last longer. This included using an aluminum or stainless steel body, scratch-resistant glass and a corrosion-resistant exhaust system. The theory was that the car would contain 45 percent steel and 40 percent light metal.

The result of the research appeared in 1973 as a somewhat unfinished-looking skeleton-type car. An argument against the Long-Life car was the belief that a consumer would pay 30 percent more than for a "regular car"—the projected cost—and that the owner would keep the car for twenty years—the projected life of the vehicle—ignoring technical advances that might be made during the vehicle's twenty-year life.

ITALDESIGN MEDICI I

The Medici was named after the famous Florence family known for its subdued elegance and business savvy. Thus, Italdesign attempted to create a vehicle with sophisticated, balanced lines.

Built over a Maserati V8 5 liter frame, the Medici I's interior housed six seats: two forward, four rear, with two facing rearward in typical limousine style. The seats were finished in light velour upholstery. The interior was well lit with the glass roof.

The vehicle was fairly long—the seat arrangement necessitated this—with a wheelbase of 124 inches and a total length of 208 inches. Its height was 54 inches.

The main criticism of the Medici was the lack of balance or consistency between the front and rear. The wedge-shaped, streamlined hood with pop-up headlights was the antithesis of the cropped-off, almost hatchback-looking rear end. Word was that even the designer, Giorgetto Giugiaro, was so displeased that he penned a sequel vehicle: the Medici II.

LAMBORGHINI BRAVO

The "little Lamborghini," as it was called in a Bertone company brochure, was one example of the clean lines of Bertone designs. Tinted glass gave an impression of no A-pillar and the set of square notches on the car's hood was actually air intakes. The Bravo, designed by Marcello Gandini, was based on the Lamborghini Uracco mechanicals, although the V8 was enlarged to 3 liters delivering 300 horsepower and a top speed of 169 mph. Wheelbase was reduced to 89 inches. Height was a mere 40 inches and length 147 inches.

The rather unsophisticated interior housed a padded dashboard encircling a thin instrument panel of brushed aluminum. For all its sharp, low stylistic lines, the Bravo had conventional opening doors. Although never put into production, the prototype was driven more than 40,000 miles.

Incidentally, the name "Bravo" or "brave" was a reference to the courageous fighting bull.

RENAULT BRV

The Renault BRV (Basic Research Vehicle) was not a dream car. It was not a styling exercise. It was simply a study in vehicle safety. The increase in emphasis on vehicle safety worldwide in the 1970s resulted in the organization of an internationally sponsored conference on Experimental Safety Vehicles, which was first held in 1971 in France. These conferences continue to this day.

The Renault studies, sponsored in part by the French government, resulted in a vehicle (the BRV) with a reinforced frame structure, collision-absorbing body rails and body panels, a specially designed seat-belt retracting system, increased interior padding, and roll-over protection. The BRV was powered by a V6 engine overhanging and driving the front wheels. It was also equipped with full independent suspension. The reinforced frame structure was adopted by many later Renault models.

VAUXHALL SRV

The Vauxhall SRV—Styling Research Vehicle—was a four door, four seater only 41 inches high. All four passengers and the engine were accommodated within the car's wheelbase. The front seats were fixed, but control pedals, steering column, and front-seat rake were adjustable to suit individual driving requirements. The fixed nature of the seats also added to the car's overall body strength. All control switches were mounted in the driver's door and were grouped in sequence, as in an aircraft cockpit.

The SRV's design incorporated some novel approaches for aerodynamic research at high speeds, such ideas as "trimming" the car in motion by the use of an aerofoil in the nose, an electric levelling system at the rear, and—following aircraft practices—a pump system to redistribute fuel load among a series of storage tanks. The body of the SRV was pillarless and molded of glass fiber reinforced with carbon fiber.

PININFARINA CR25

The name CR25 was derived from the impressive drag coefficient figure achieved: 0.256. The development of the vehicle proved a point long held by Pininfarina that functional design (read: aerodynamical design) can lead to a good-looking vehicle.

The thick band circling the vehicle not only protects the body, but also serves as a stabilizer with negative lift. The rear of the vehicle featured automatically operated aero-dynamic brakes. Particular attention focused on body smoothness, with very little ornamentation: Note the lack of side mirrors, the use of pop-up headlights, and the missing door handles. The side windows were even immobile. The door handles were replaced with an electric device that permitted actuation of the doors with a simple touch. This feature was patented by Pininfarina. Ferrari parts were used solely in the vehicle's construction.

ALFA ROMEO EAGLE

The Eagle originated from the hands of Pininfarina, who took an Alfa Romeo Alfetta GT chassis and created a two-seat coupe convertible with a removable hard top. The wedge shape and roll bar were a resurrected scheme found on the 1968 Alfa Romeo P33 and 1971 Alfa Romeo P33 Spider, also bodied by Pininfarina. The roll bar actually extended from behind the passenger compartment, around the doors, and continued toward the front end, providing a stiff occupant area. The goal was to show that an open car could be produced with passive safety in mind.

The interior trim was replete with blue velvet. Even the steering wheel was finished in the velvet trim. Instrumentation was digital and controls were touch control—gently sliding up or down—and mounted on the center console.

One feature probably not designed for passive safety was the color combination: a blue interior and a red exterior. But the car was certainly highly visible.

OPEL GT2

This 2 + 2 concept from Opel was designed with fuel economy, roadholding, passenger accommodations, and handling in mind. The low, sharp nose helped the fuel economy numbers by producing good aerodynamics. Built over Opel Manta GT/E mechanicals, the GT2 was capable of 124 mph.

The car was equipped with sliding doors and very aerodynamically unobtrusive side-view mirrors. Further emphasizing the flush look, the door handles were placed at the base of the wide mirrors. The larger part of the side windows was immovable, while a smaller part could be lowered and raised independently. This window arrangement became more and more popular during the 1970s and '80s. The two rear seats could fold flat.

ALFA ROMEO NAVAJO

The main purpose of the two-seat Bertone Navajo was to study aerodynamics for roadholding rather than pure speed. In the process the vehicle received some accolades on its styling: the car was dubbed "Star of the Auto Expo" at the Los Angeles Auto Show in 1976.

The front spoiler of the Navajo was automatically adjusted and the huge rear spoiler was, if nothing else, a major eye-catching feature of the vehicle. The headlights were atypical in that they popped out from the side of the vehicle rather than the hood top. The interior featured a digital instrument panel and gauges on every engine activity possible. A meter even displayed the amount of lateral "Gs" felt in cornering.

The Navajo was based on an Alfa Romeo T33 sports racing chassis—therefore the right-hand steering—with a mid-mounted flat V12 engine.

FERRARI RAINBOW

The Ferrari Rainbow can claim a feat that goes beyond performance figures and styling lines: it was the only Ferrari ever sold through a department store catalog. In 1979 Marshall Field offered the Bertone-styled Rainbow in their holiday catalog. The price for this one-of-a-kind gift for the man who has everything: $250,000.

A convertible by definition, the Rainbow featured a retractable steel top—rather than the conventional fabric—that slid over the passengers during the rainy season and then tucked itself back behind the seats when the sun chose to shine. The chassis was that of a Ferrari Dino 308 GT cut short by 4 inches. Power was from a 250 horsepower V8 engine. This very compact vehicle had a front grille that also served as a bumper. The Rainbow first appeared in white but was later modeled at the 1977 Frankfurt show in a light blue body. By the way . . . no takers for the catalog offer. It's possible the shipping and handling charges were a bit excessive.

ITALDESIGN MEDICI II

The Medici II was the result of designer Giugiaro's dissatisfaction with the Medici I of 1974. Gone from the Medici II were the sloped nose and pop-up headlights of the Medici I. Replacing them were a flatter nose with a distinct radiator grille and rectangular headlights. This move created a better balance between front and rear.

The interior was also refigured with the facing seats replaced with two individual forward-facing seats split by a wide armrest. The interior also provided the obligatory limousine accessories: a cabinet housing bar, refrigerator, desk, television, and telephone. The velour upholstery of the Medici I was replaced with leather.

All exterior dimensions remained the same: wheelbase 124 inches, total length 208 inches, and height 54 inches. The V8 Maserati engine also remained in place.

MERCEDES-BENZ C111-IID

The year 1976 saw the return of the Mercedes-Benz Experimental "C." Taking the old C111-II body, the new C111-IID was designed with the express intent to break records. The major redesign replaced the Wankel rotary engine with a 5 cylinder diesel engine. Hence the "D" designation. Turbocharging was also added, more than doubling the horsepower from 80 to 190. Other modifications to the car included fitting the headlights into the mud guard under a plexiglass cover to improve aerodynamics and the addition of high-speed radial tires. Two fuel tanks in the doors were enlarged to 15.5 gallons as Mercedes set its eyes on the long-distance driving records. Pit stops were even rehearsed and lowered to ten seconds.

The preparation did not go unrewarded. In 1976 a team of four drivers changing every 2.5 hours went on to set long-distance world records on the Nardo track in Italy. The records were: 156.867 for 5000 miles; 156.676 for 10,000 km; and 156.396 for 10,000 miles. Other records established were averaging 157.525 mph over 12 hours and 157.161 mph over 24 hours.

PEUGETTE 104

In a book full of exotic designs and wild technology, the Peugette 104 stands out not for its ground-breaking aerodynamic style, but for quite the opposite, in fact. While most car designers would view a comment that a car looks the same coming as going as an insult, the designers of this vehicle would simply nod in agreement; it was designed that way.

The Peugette 104, designed by Pininfarina and built on a Peugeot 104 floor pan, was a study in cost cutting. In an experiment to cut costs, the front and back parts were identical, as were the doors. The argument was, the fewer parts required, the lower the cost. Unfortunately, the corollary of the argument was, the fewer the parts, the less visually appealing the design.

The interior was sparse and had an untraditional instrument panel: none. The gauges were housed in small black boxes secured to the top of a padded dashboard.

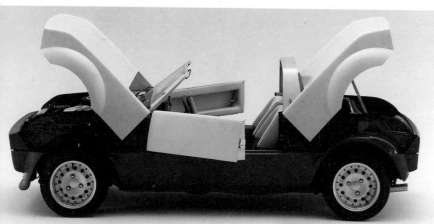

FIAT ECOS

The Ecos was an electrically powered vehicle developed jointly by Fiat and Pininfarina. The purpose was to design an electric car that had room for more than just 2–3 passengers while still providing good luggage space. The rear seats of the Ecos folded in half and flipped forward, securing the entire seat in the area usually available for the rear passenger's feet. This arrangement provided additional rear cargo space. The battery packs supplying the 35 horsepower engine were below the front and rear seats giving the passengers more room.

The design was far more functional than aesthetic—very high but with a very short wheelbase—but that was the norm of alternative fuel vehicles of the day.

FORD GHIA GTK

The Ford Fiesta GTK, developed by Ghia, was designed to meet the objectives of an elegant, futuristic, and aerodynamic vehicle that also provided maximum interior space and sufficient luggage space. What resulted was the longest Fiesta in the world.

Built on an extended Fiesta wheelbase (from 90 to 94 inches), the GTK—Grand Touring Kombi (a German word for station wagon)—was a progression from the Granada and Taunus-based Megastar I and II concept vehicles developed years earlier.

The headlamps of the GTK were behind electrically controlled panels. Ducts in front of these panels collected air from beneath the front spoiler and channelled it over the hood and roof of the vehicle. Lower body panels were designed to generate a ground effect for improved high-speed handling.

The door windows were opened electrically, and the rear-quarter windows were hinged at the leading edge. For added visibility, fixed glass panels were built into the center pillars.

The vehicle also featured an on-board computer and electronic digital-display instruments that provided travel information as well as road speed, engine speed, and the other driver information.

GHIA TUAREG

The Ghia Tuareg was one vehicle that may have crossed the line between concept and production model. Although never produced in numbers, the Tuareg aroused so much interest at its debut at the 1978 Geneva Motor Show a Ford dealer in Germany offered replicas for sale. Since the off-roader was based on the production Ford Fiesta, the conversion was not too complicated, although the dealer had to base his replicas solely on photos of the original.

Alterations to the production Fiesta needed to create the Tuareg included the change in engine ventilation for desert conditions (five extra louvers were built into the hood), enlarged wheel arches that converted to running boards, larger tires, stiffer suspension, and a wider rear track. Roll-over protection for the occupants was provided by a special steel hoop integrated into the roof and center pillars. An adjustable halogen roof-mounted spotlight, a heavy-duty roof rack for fuel and water containers, and a strengthened tubular steel front and rear bumper were further testimony that this was an off-roader. The vehicle also featured a split rear tailgate and fold-down rear seats. Heavy, durable material was utilized for the seats and floor.

JAGUAR XJS SPIDER

Part of the final design of the Jaguar XJS was a result of an effort to utilize the aerodynamic lessons learned in the wind tunnel with the 1978 Pininfarina CNR. Part of that lesson was adopted with the bumperless look and pop-up headlights. The round lines of this 1978 XJS elicited memories of the earlier Jaguar D- and E-Types.

The interior was simple and designed so because of safety concerns: the fewer protruding levers and knobs, the fewer to distract the driver during driving and injure the driver in a collision. Instruments were of the LED type. The instrument panel was completely black when the vehicle was not running. The center transmission tunnel merged into the console forming a small cocoon for each passenger. The lift-off targa top section could be stored in the car's trunk and behind the central roll hoop was a detachable, small hood section.

Almost every automobile enthusiast magazine in the late 70s published articles praising the design and imploring Jaguar to produce the machine. But it never happened.

LANCIA SIBLIO

With the Siblio, the designers at Bertone set out to integrate what was known as the car's volumes, i.e., the body, windows, and bumpers. By using tinted windows made of plastic and rounded body features, it was difficult to discern where sheet metal ended and glass began. Plastic windows were used because the glass supplier could not meet the deadline for the 1978 Turin Auto Show.

The interior contained a solid steering wheel and digital instrumentation in the driver's direct sight. The steering wheel was anatomically designed with a thick square rim, a channel on the front surface to accommodate the thumb, and a deep groove behind for the fingers. Various controls were housed on the inside of the wheel. The wiper system was unique in that it used a single wiper attached to a geared rack which vertically swept the window. The only moveable portion of the side windows was a small circular hole on each side which popped out and slid back.

The Siblio utilized the Lancia Stratos V6 layout but added 3.9 inches in wheelbase. The vehicle was the last car built around the Ferrari Dino V6 engine.

MERCEDES-BENZ C111-III

For the first time, the Mercedes experimental "C" took on more of a purely experimental look. All previous models still held a bit of the road car appearance; the C111-III disposed of that. The wheelbase was increased by 4 inches to 107, the front track narrowed to 50 inches, and the rear narrowed to 52 inches. Total vehicle length was 212 inches.

Utilizing the turbo-charged diesel from the C111-IID,

Mercedes boosted output to 230 horsepower and added a wind-tunnel honed body. It was this body, with nary a crease, fully covered wheels, and a rear fin, that brought the vehicle into the true test-vehicle realm. The vehicle's drag coefficient was below 0.2.

More speed records fell under the Mercedes experimentals with the C111-III capturing nine world records including an average of 198.994 mph for 100 miles, 198.983 mph for 1000 miles, and 195.319 mph over 12 hours. Fuel economy during the 12 hours was an amazing 17.6 mpg.

PININFARINA CNR

As a theoretical-experiment vehicle, the CNR tested optimum aerodynamics at Pininfarina. The 1:1 scale version of the first tested CNR in 1976 yielded a drag coefficient of 0.160. After construction of systems for engine cooling and passenger compartment ventilation, the coefficient rose to 0.172. A theoretic number of 0.230 was reached when including typical vehicle running—still an impressive number. Pininfarina predicted fuel savings of up to 15 percent for a family vehicle of this design.

A more finished vehicle was produced in 1990, the CNR E2, that utilized some of the findings of this experimental form. The 1978 Jaguar XJS by Pininfarina also exhibits some of the lines discovered in this wind-tunnel test model.

MERCEDES-BENZ C111-IV

The speed tests continued in 1970 at Mercedes-Benz with the C111-IV. Five speed records were set in this vehicle at the Nardo track in Italy. One record was a single lap at more than 250 mph, eclipsing the previous mark of 221 mph held by a Porsche 917 CanAm. This "C" car was powered by a V8 twin turbo-charged engine developing 500 horsepower.

The C111-IV differentiated itself from the C111-III by its large front spoiler and two vertical fins at the rear. Initial tests were intended primarily to study the effects of fins and spoilers on aerodynamics at speeds in excess of 248 mph. The two rear fins controlled crosswinds. The asymmetrical front and rear spoilers provided greater down force. The C111-IV was constructed of glass-fiber synthetic materials with carbon and boron fiber reinforcements.

The C111-IV was only capable of shattering a few records due to the fact that Michelin could not guarantee the tires for more than thirty minutes at speeds in excess of 250 mph and lateral Gs greater than .4. Four more records did fall in thirty minutes with the C111-IV covering 10 km at 199.140 mph, 10 miles at 207.114 mph, 100 km at 233.335 mph, and 100 miles at 228.196 mph.

RENAULT EPURE

Renault's second full-scale study of vehicle safety (the BRV was the first) was the EPURE (Etude de la Protection des Usagers de la Route et de l'Environnement). Based on the Renault 5, the EPURE implemented safety features like energy-absorbing front and rear ends, a strengthened passenger compartment, enhanced impact zones for better occupant protection in front and rear collisions, a collapsible steering column, and greater roof strength via roll-over members. Interior padding was also at a maximum.

Also highly considered in front-end design were pedestrian impacts. To lessen the chance of severe pedestrian injury the EPURE featured a deformable hood, increased distance between hood and stiff vehicle parts, covered wiper shafts, and a protective cap over the top of shock absorbers.

RENAULT EVE

Simply stated, the EVE was a study in fuel economy. Renault developed the EVE (Economy Vehicle Elements) following an agreement with the French government's Energy Saving Agency.

The goal of this rolling experimental lab was to evaluate a finite number of factors in the fuel-economy formula, namely, aerodynamics and engine and transmission management.

Aerodynamic investigation centered on creating a usable medium-size area (i.e., good passenger space, cargo space, comfort, safety, and performance) while optimizing the body's coefficient of drag, thus influencing fuel economy. The final air-resistance figure achieved by the EVE was 0.239. Engine and transmission management meant the use of electronics to create an optimum combination of transmission-gear ratio and engine throttle openings. The instrumentation was composed of two electronic graphs which showed the power curve and the fuel consumption curve allowing maximum engine efficiency.

The experiment was successful in creating a car that posted fuel-economy figures better than the norm of the day: 68.9 mpg at 56 mph; 51.3 mpg at 75 mph; and 42.8 mpg city. Top speed was 104 mph.

VOLVO LCP 2000

Unlike many of the "car of the future" projects underway at the time, Volvo's LCP (Light Component Project) 2000 program was a bit different because it not only sought a car with good fuel consumption, but one that would follow the guidelines of "minimization of lifetime energy," i.e., keep low the total energy consumption for raw materials, production, use of vehicle, and recovery of materials, while still satisfying consumer demand.

The LCP 2000, built in cooperation with the British design firm I.A.D., was a station wagon-type vehicle with two front seats and two rear-facing rear seats. A reinforce-ment tunnel ran the width of the vehicle between the two rows of seats, providing greater body rigidity. The two rear seats were accessible through the rear gate, which hinged nearly midway up to the roof area. Either rear seat could fold flat to increase luggage capacity. The interior instrumentation was modest, with a set of dials grouped directly behind the steering wheel. The driver seat as well as the steering column and instrument panel were adjustable. Power originated from a turbo-charged 3 cylinder direct-injection diesel engine. Four LCP 2000 Volvos were constructed over the life of the program.

VOLVO TUNDRA

The Tundra was a new collaboration between the Swedish maker Volvo and the Italian Bertone. Built around Volvo 343 mechanicals, the Tundra may be the most production-like vehicle produced by Bertone in the 70s and early 80s. This three-door was lower and wider in the center than the production 343. Although Volvo chose not to utilize the Tundra's styling cues, Citroën did in its BX.

The Tundra was a four-seat sedan with modest lines. The window look—glass and pillars blended together—was a carry-over from the Bertone Siblio. But the notched roof line over the rear side window was a bit unusual. A bit more boxlike than previous and proceeding Bertone attempts, the Tundra still featured an extensive glass area. The energy-absorbent bumpers were emphasized with a color different from the car body.

The instrument panel consisted of a vertical bar graph and lighting-alert system: green, all systems O.K.; white, not.

ASTON MARTIN BULLDOG

Started as a private project, the Bulldog eventually was taken in house at Aston Martin, and produced in about only twelve months. The aluminum-bodied car penned by William Towns consisted of very flat panels and glasswork. At only 43 inches high, the gull-wing doors were a necessity for passenger entrance and exit. Padded handles on each side and the rounding of the base of the doors allowed the passengers a bit more assistance. The interior featured leather seats, burr walnut panelling, LCD digital instrumentation, custom-made air conditioning (the windows were fixed, so this was a requirement), and stereo/cassette. Overall, the interior was quite modest, with few switches and levers.

The mid-mounted 5.3 liter twin-turbo engine was mated to a 5 speed transmission. The chassis was a multi-tubular design with backbone and integral roll-over bar, diagonally braced. Four aluminum safety fuel tanks were placed symmetrically at the car's center, thereby eliminating any effect varying fuel load would have on handling. The five quartz headlights were concealed under a movable panel on the hood. Lacking for a road car were side mirrors.

Top speed of the Bulldog was estimated at 193 mph, although the vehicle never reached that speed under the supervision of Aston Martin. It seems, so the story goes, that just as the vehicle was being readied for high-speed testing on the European continent in 1981, a gentleman arrived with a case (Gucci) full of traveler's checks and departed with the Bulldog.

BERTONE ATHON

The Athon was designed as a bit of a tribute to Lamborghini, which faced financial trouble during the early 1980s. Powering the Athon was the Lamborghini 3 liter V8 from the Urraco production model.

A pure speedster design, the Athon had no provision for a roof or fold-down top. The engine lid opened transversely and a deep, narrow luggage compartment was designed behind the seats.

The steering wheel resembled a rope lasso with the spoke from the steering column mounted in a single spot—approximately the 7 o'clock position—on the wheel. The transmission shift lever looked like the handle of a large wooden-handled knife. Main interior controls were grouped on a unit to the left of the steering wheel. The instrument panel combined LED technology with a graph-like display. The stereo system was incorporated into the door panel. The car was also equipped with a computer.

Just a bit of trivia: the name Athon was another name of the Egyptian pharaoh Amenhotep IV (1377–1358 B.C.), who introduced the cult of Athon, or hymn to the sun.

FERRARI PININ

A four-door Ferrari? It took a bit of persuading by Pininfarina, but eventually Enzo Ferrari allowed the experiment. The car was named after the founder of Pininfarina and presented on the company's fiftieth anniversary at the Turin Motor Show.

Even with the two extra doors, the Pinin was still not designed to be a typical sedan. A large glass area, sport wheels, and a large radiator indicated the car was more than a sedan. The 5 liter horizontally opposed 12 cylinders also told that this was more than sedate wheels. Special multi-parabolic headlights were utilized, which used reflecting surfaces for better intensity. When not lit, the rear lights matched the car's body color. The front wipers were concealed under a flap that remained closed until the wipers were engaged. The windows were fixed shut. In the interior, all important instruments were placed directly in front of the driver. Not to let the rear passengers feel alone, a radio and headsets along with a telephone were fitted for the rear.

1 9 8 0

GHIA GRANADA ALTAIR

Taking the production chassis of the Ford Granada and adding only 2 inches in length, cutting 3 inches in height and 4 inches in width, Ghia created the Altair, an experimental, five-seat, four-door sedan.

The Altair had a respectable drag coefficient of .35, aided by its low lines and sharp front end. The four head-lights and two auxiliary lamps were all recessed behind a clear plastic shield.

The most eye-catching feature of the Altair was the see-through bronze-tinted plexiglass panels built into each

door to increase visibility and the feeling of spaciousness. The bronze line was also used to mask the recessed door handles and the air extraction vents for air conditioning and fresh air ventilation systems. The front and rear ends incor-porated impact-absorbent bumpers. The side-mounted mirrors were remotely controlled and a single wiper cleared the entire front windshield.

The Altair used a regular production model's 2.8 liter fuel-injected V6 engine. It had independent front and rear suspension, low-profile tires, and stereo sound system.

ITALDESIGN MEDUSA

Built over a Lancia Montecarlo 2000 chassis, the Medusa sought to meld the concerns of aerodynamics and interior space—a much-researched topic. The rear mounting of the engine was unusual for a sedan of this type, but allowed ample profiling of the front end.

The Medusa achieved a drag coefficient of 0.263 with the aid of flush styling. For example, the side windows, fixed and flush with the outside framework, opened by electrically operated sliding panes: the moving part slid forward and receded internally. Door handles, side mirror, and wheel covers were also designed for optimum aerodynamics.

A great deal of research led to the interior control layout. All buttons and levers were concentrated onto a single unit at the center of the steering column. The unit could change position for the driver's comfort. The push buttons transmitted commands not via cables, but through ultrasound. The stereo boasted two speakers per passenger, located inside the headrests for the front seats and inside the seat back for the rear passengers. A special remote-control device made it possible either to turn off the lights or turn on the parking lights from a distance.

Greater interior space was provided by lessening the vehicle's luggage capacity and the positioning of the rear wheels well behind the rear seats.

PEUGEOT VERA PROJECT

Between 1980 and 1983 Peugeot built four prototypes under the acronym VERA (Véhicule Econome de Recherche Appliquée, or "Applied Research Economy Vehicle"). Sponsored by the French government Agency for Energy Conservation, the vehicle studies were meant to stimulate development of fuel-efficient vehicles. Target fuel consumption was set at 40.4 mpg, a 25 percent reduction from 29.7 mpg. The main areas of concern were: weight reduction, aerodynamics, and fuel efficiency.

The VERA 01 was the first vehicle constructed over the chassis of the Peugeot 305. It was powered by a gasoline engine and achieved a weight reduction of 188 kg off the production 305. The coefficient of drag was 0.305. It improved fuel economy by 26 percent.

The VERA 02 was fitted with a diesel engine. The goal with the diesel engine was to achieve better fuel economy than the standard gasoline Peugeot 305GL. The VERA 02 was capable of a top speed of 98 mph. It reduced weight by 185 pounds over the 305 and achieved a coefficient of 0.316. Fuel consumption was reduced by 45 percent over the gasoline 305GL.

The final two prototypes in the VERA project never reached fruition because of a cut in funding from the French government. Although never realized, the final two prototypes were to test one major technology: direct-injection diesel engines. Although never run, the VERA PLUS, and then the VERA PROFIL in 1983, featured bodies different from the previous two VERA experiments.

The interior space of the VERA PLUS remained the same as the 305 but was 2.8 inches shorter, thus reducing weight. Weight saving was also achieved by the improved layout of the interior instruments and the use of digital gauges.

The final VERA prototype, the VERA PROFIL, was even more stylistic than the VERA PLUS, with its semi-covered rear wheels. Power for the VERA PROFIL was to come from a direct-injection diesel engine. Output would be 41 horsepower with a projected fuel economy of 66 mpg.

Even without the motorized PLUS and PROFIL, direct-inject diesel engines have been ruled out for consumer-orientated vehicles because of their noise.

VOLKSWAGEN AUTO 2000

The 2000 nomenclature on the AUTO 2000—actually the name of a program sponsored by the German government (Mercedes-Benz too had an AUTO 2000 vehicle)—was to designate the future look of the concept: the year 2000. But it could have just as easily been an index of the number of companies involved in the car project along with Volkswagen. In cooperation with many auto suppliers, Volkswagen set out to address many issues, fuel economy, exhaust emissions, safety, and comfort being some of them.

In response to these elements, Volkswagen produced a mid-class vehicle with two engine options: diesel and spark engine. A redesigned ventilation system—fresh air entered the vehicle through a vaned grille between the engine hood and the front side panel rather than from the windscreen—was a control system designed to achieve desired interior temperature as quickly as possible to increase driver and passenger comfort. The digital instrumentation was very large and easy to read, a definite safety feature. The AUTO 2000 also utilized the ALI navigation system. An anti-lock brake system (ABS) along with a navigation system provided safety for occupants. Maximum speed was 93 mph. The plastic tailgate and wheel-housing liners and seats could be recycled. With the 3 cylinder diesel engine, the AUTO 2000 topped out at 93 mph and had a fuel economy figure of 71 mpg.

VOLVO CONCEPT CAR

Not much of an original name or ground breaking in style, the Volvo Concept Car (VCC) was a Volvo view of the car of the 1980s. Emphasizing efficient fuel consumption, comfort, convenience, and safety, the VCC featured: an automatically retractable spoiler to enhance aerodynamics—the spoiler lowered at speeds in excess of 42 mph; lightweight materials; a turbo diesel engine; a malfunction warning system comprised of cathode ray tubes; a new automatic-leveling rear suspension designed to provide comfort, suppress exterior noise, and adjust to varying luggage and occupant loads; a motorized passive safety belt; and a pressed recess in the floor plate that, together with the stuffing in the seat cushion, pushed the passenger during a collision against the seat instead of under the seat belt. The edge of the tailgate was recessed into the roof, allowing easier package loading and unloading.

The body design concept was used on the Volvo 760.

VOLKSWAGEN ARVW

With a drag coefficient of 0.15—a typical sleek production car has a drag coefficient of .30—and powered by a modified 2.4 liter 6 cylinder diesel engine, the Volkswagen ARVW (Aerodynamic Research Volkswagen) was capable of a top speed of 225 mph and 30 mpg. Modifications to the engine included the addition of a turbocharger, low-compression pistons, and increased piston cooling.

The single-seat Volkswagen was developed as a test bed for aerodynamic research as well as a mull for testing directional stability, front-end lift, engine cooling without minimal engine power loss, and mechanical resistance.

AC GHIA

The AC Ghia was a concept design for a luxury mid-engine two-seat sports car. Powered by a Ford 3.0 liter V6 engine and constructed over the AC Cars M.E. 3000 chassis, the AC Ghia developed further on the Action racing prototype introduced in 1978.

A very low front end housed two sets of headlamps: one recessed into the front spoiler and the other set behind protective rotating flaps in the front fenders. The wedge-shaped vehicle had fairly good rear visibility, with special cutouts in the rear pillars. Wide ducts cut into the vehicle's side provided air cooling to the engine and brakes. An insulated luggage area was located beneath the rear aerofoil behind the engine compartment.

Overall height of the car was 48 inches, with a total length of 12 feet 5 inches.

AUDI QUARTZ

The Pininfarina-designed Audi Quartz was a 2+2 coupe with four-wheel drive. The main goal behind the design was to display the stylistic possibilities of a vehicle built of light metal and non-metal materials. The materials utilized on the Quartz—Kevlar, carbon fiber, metal/plastic laminate and polycarbonate—were the norm for aerospace applications, but not automobile. The front and rear bumpers were made of a Kevlar/honeycomb/Kevlar sandwich, the engine hood was aluminum, the door panels were a steel/polypropylene/steel sandwich, and the seat frames and steering wheel were made of carbon fiber.

The split along the body side was actually functional, as it guided air into a slot in the vehicle's front and out a slot behind the front wheel arches and then down the body side. The door handles were concealed behind a slot at the rear of the side windows. The tiny headlights were a result of a study by the company Carello on elliptical optics. Slots in the side mirrors provided interior ventilation. With a good power to weight ratio, the 2.2 liter 200 horsepower turbo Quartz had ample speed.

The Quartz receives the award for the best incorporation of manufacturer's logo into a functional item with its use of the fourth Audi ring as the gas filler cover and the four-ring Audi-type exhaust pipes outlined in red.

The vehicle was dedicated to the Swiss magazine *Revue Automobile* on the occasion of its 75th anniversary.

CITROEN XENIA

The Xenia four-passenger wagon was designed with the American market in mind. But, to date, no such vehicle from Citroën has entered the U.S. market. And maybe that is a good idea, considering the glut of minivan-type vehicles already there.

The exterior styling of the Xenia was very clean, with loads of glass and a straight body line set over the 168 inch vehicle length. Vehicle height was a slight 49 inches. The low cowl line (the point where the windshield and hood meet) and the low side-glass line translated to good driver visibility. The low cowl line also served a functional purpose beyond visibility. At the base of the windshield sat a group of solar battery cells which produced energy for the in-car entertainment and comfort system when the vehicle was not running.

The interior was divided up into sections by a central tunnel. The seat backs were pear-shaped and very thin. Controls were set within easy reach in a curved arrangement just behind the steering wheel. This design concealed the small instrument panel from all except the driver. To keep the rear passengers busy since they could not see the instrument panel, a small monitor for video games was installed on the rear section of the center tunnel. The vehicle was also equipped with an intercom and a telephone.

GHIA AVANT GARDE

Taking the Ford Escort base, Ghia built a sleek vehicle named the Avant Garde. As with most design studies of the 1980s, the Avant Garde spent much time in the wind tunnel. The car's under side was smoothed, the windshield was raked at 67 degrees to vertical, twin cooling ducts for the engine were positioned between the front bumper and hood while the headlights and front direction indicators were partially recessed behind rotating panels to improve airflow. The opening rear window was fitted with an aerofoil.

The interior was lined in hand-finished suede and leather. The electronic instruments were recessed to avoid reflections while the controls for direction indicators, horn, and wipers were situated at points directly behind the steering wheel. A security feature of the vehicle allowed the radio to be removed and a carpet blind to be drawn forward over the interior.

The most low-tech, but nonetheless notable, features of the Avant Garde were the removable suede shoulder bags integrated into the door design.

OPEL TECH I

The Opel Tech I was one of the many concepts to be born of the wind tunnel. This sleek four-door achieved a drag coefficient of 0.235 due in part to the special attention paid to the design of the under body and wheel rims. The special design also aided in brake cooling. An intriguing feature of the Tech I involved the license plate; at various speeds, the plate would move up or down, adjusting the amount of air flow into the engine compartment.

The Tech I was based on the Kadett front-wheel-drive platform. The interior featured four wraparound seats, digital instrumentation, and touch-sensitive controls placed near the driver.

1 9 8 1

MERCEDES-BENZ AUTO 2000

As with other concept cars of its day, the Mercedes-Benz 2000 was an experiment devoted to designing a car to meet the demands of a more fuel-efficient and safety-conscious society of the future—keeping in mind that the same society still desires a good-looking, comfortable vehicle.

The AUTO 2000 combined generous interior space, climate control, noise insulation, sufficient storage space, high towing capacity, and good fuel economy. The car was tested with gas turbine, V8 gas, and turbo V6 diesel engines. The twin-turbo diesel delivered 35 mpg. An unusual engineering choice hinged the front hood at the side. The doors were constructed of aluminum and the nose of fiberglass, helping reduce weight by 50 percent over the production S-Class Mercedes-Benz. Unique to this Mercedes was the independent mini windows for the front occupants and the bulbous rear window and hatchback look. Curiously lacking for a car with a safety emphasis is the right side mirror. The AUTO 2000 program was initiated by the German government and also included a vehicle from Volkswagen: the 1980 Volkswagen AUTO 2000.

GHIA BREZZA

The mid-engine Brezza was constructed on the floor pan of the North American Ford EXP two-seater, an Escort derivative. Powering the sleek vehicle was the Escort 1.6 liter engine mounted in the rear position. Designed with maximum aerodynamics in mind, the Brezza utilized skirted rear wheels, retractable headlights, and a partial belly-pan and fairings ahead of the front and rear wheels to smooth airflow underneath the car. This under body airflow was used to extract cooling air from the fully ducted radiator, which took in air through slots beneath the vehicle's nose.

Further promoting the vehicle's aerodynamics—a drag coefficient of .30 was achieved—the side windows were electrically operated and ran in specially developed channels that allowed the window frames to be almost flush with the body sides.

Luggage was accommodated at both front and rear, with extra storage for small packages behind the seats.

ITALDESIGN CAPSULA

A van, passenger car, or cargo van? Maybe all of the above.

With the Capsula, Italdesign presented a proposal for a vehicle consisting of a flexible platform that included the engine, transmission parts, fuel tank, spare wheel, luggage area, power brake, heater, and front and rear lamp clusters that could accommodate various types of body styles. Simply plop a new "cap" onto the base and create an ambulance, or even a tow truck. The Capsula was based on the engineering of the Alfa Romeo Alfasud Boxer.

In the passenger-car configuration, 80 percent of the vehicle's length was occupant space. The doors were gull-wing and provided easy entrance and exit to both front and rear passengers. There were no window-lowering mechanisms for the side windows; instead, the windows slid forward and back. There was no rear hatch. The front seats swiveled and the rear seats could slide as well as fold. All essential driving controls—including speedometer—were built into the steering wheel. The instrument console that housed the push-button automatic transmission was mobile, capable of sliding forward, allowing more interior space.

SBARRO SUPER TWELVE

The name Super Twelve was a direct relation to the number of cylinders under the vehicle's hood. What the name doesn't explain was the way these cylinders were created. The designer, Franco Sbarro, joined two Kawasaki 1300 cc 6 cylinder motorcycle engines and placed them in the midship position, creating a 240 horsepower powerplant. The inventive engine construction propelled the 126 inch, plastic-bodied Super Twelve from 0 to 100 mph in 8 seconds. The two-seat interior was lined in leather and instrumentation was doubled for each engine except for the speedometer. The rear hatch opened to reveal a hinged door covering the engine. The two-tone color of the Super Twelve was fascinating as well. Rather than the typical horizontally split two-color scheme, Sbarro chose to blend the color change gradually from front (white) to rear (bright red).

VOLKSWAGEN STUDENT

Like many concept vehicles of its time, the VW Student research prototype was developed in part to address the concern of fuel economy. The 50 horsepower engine, derived from a standard Volkswagen Polo, allowed a top speed of 98 mph with fuel economy of 47 mpg. With a 123 inch length the Student was a sub-compact, or as the British say, a "mini."

A new front seat was developed so that more space became available for rear-seat occupants. The rear seats could be folded down, providing a luggage compartment. All instrumentation was digital.

Despite its diminutive length the car still provided collision protection front and rear, as well as large doors. The coefficient of drag was quite respectable at 0.31 for a car so short.

BERTONE DELFINO

The Delfino, or "Dolphin," was based on the Alfa Romeo 6 sedan but with a wider track and reduced overhang. Power came from a 157 horsepower 6 cylinder engine. Top speed of the 2+2 coupe was 137 mph.

The most eye-catching exterior portion of the Delfino was the altered waist line (the area where the window and body meet) with the high trunk and flush glass treatment. The headlights were of the pop-up variety and the small

Alfa Romeo grille fit in just fine on the facia. The interior had not so much a steering column but a steering panel. Rather than mounting the steering wheel to a column, the wheel sat in the middle of a protruding control panel which ran from the driver's door to the center console, where it was secured. The vehicle's LED analog-style gauges sat behind the control panel.

VOLANIS HELIOS

The former Matra designer-turned-independent-stylist, Antoine Volanis, created the Helios through his French design firm Design Volanis. In this wagon/car hybrid, the efficient implementation of safety and comfort were emphasized. Controls were centered around a double-handled steering device ("steering wheel" being a misnomer), thus keeping the driver in better control of the vehicle. The four individual contoured seats—a common design feature of Volanis vehicles—divided by a central tunnel provided the comfort.

As with Volanis' later design, the 1984 Apollon, aerodynamics were also addressed. The smooth exterior with flush headlights and a lack of obtrusions contributed to the low coefficient of drag of 0.22. The side mirrors were a bit atypical, mounted on the side-window glass rather than the front pillar or door. The emphasis on glass was evident on this 157 inch vehicle with a low glass line along the body side and a fully glass rear gate. A line of thin red taillights formed a half circle around the rear gate.

The overall design form shows similarities to the production Renault Espace, which Volanis designed while with Matra.

ZAGATO PROTOTIPO CHICANE

This vehicle was an example of what many designers thought the direction the automobile was headed: the multi-functional chassis. What the Chicane provided was a vehicle base that could accommodate various body styles. A flexible chassis like this was attractive for one main reason: by allowing many different-looking vehicles to make use of the same chassis, development costs were reduced. In the case of the Chicane, a 2000 cc engine could be placed either in the rear position or centrally. A mass-produced, or even one-off plastic body would then be set in place. Although this particular example may not be too attractive with its angular rear and covered rear wheels, a Chicane-type vehicle has been proposed before—1982 Italdesign Capsula and, to a certain extent, the 1976 Pininfarina Peugette 104—and it may come again.

PININFARINA COUPE

The Pininfarina Coupe, also known as the Brio, depending on which auto show it appeared in, was built on Fiat Ritmo Abarth 125 TC mechanicals. The vehicle was quite aerodynamic (coefficient of drag: 0.29) and had the window-within-a-window feature: A small portion of the side window would roll down independent of the full window. This provided ventilation without excess wind noise. Aerodynamics influenced other features of the Coupe such as concealment of the headlight wipers and rear wiper in the bumper and spoiler, respectively. Further evidence of the slippery theme was hiding the fuel filler cap beneath a flap just behind the rear wheel and the location of the door handles at a spot with the B-pillar, between the two side windows. The slots cut into the front fenders allowed heat to escape the engine compartment.

Instrumentation consisted of both analog and digital gauges, with speed and RPM information displayed via two horizontal gauges. The instrument panel tilted along with the steering column. A peculiar design feature of the interior was the choice of a V-shaped tray dashboard—sarcastically referred to as the "trash bin" style by some journalists—rather than the typical flat style.

CITROEN ECO 2000

Citroën's attempt to construct the optimum vehicle of the future took shape in the ECO 2000 program supported by the French government. The German government created its own project, AUTO 2000 (Volkswagen AUTO 2000, Mercedes-Benz AUTO 2000) but it emphasized mid-range-size cars rather than the small cars of the ECO 2000 program. The goals of the French program, begun in 1981, were: achieve an average fuel economy of 3 liter/100 km (94.2 mpg British Imperial gallon, 79 mpg U.S. gallon); provide comfortable space for four people; provide a high level of ride, handling, and braking; display acceptable

styling; and conform to all legal requirements.

The project consisted of three versions: the SA 103, SA 117, and SA 109. The first version, the SA 103, a rear-engine, rear-drive vehicle, achieved a fuel economy of 3.5 liter per 100 km (80.7 mpg British Imperial gallon, 68 mpg U.S. gallon), with a 704 cc engine. Coefficient of drag was 0.267.

The second version, the SA 117, performed the best of the three, posting fuel economy of 3.0 liter per 100 km, thus reaching the project's target fuel-economy figure. The SA 117 utilized front-wheel drive and the same 704 cc engine. Although 2.3 percent heavier than its predecessor, the SA 117 could reach 88 mph.

The final version, the SA 109 (pictured here), using a 3 cylinder, 35 horsepower engine, posted the same fuel economy as the SA 103: 3.5 liters per 100 km (80.7 mpg British Imperial gallon, 68 mpg U.S. gallon). Glass on the SA 109 was very thin (0.126 inch) and body parts were reduced to 85. It weighed a mere 880 pounds. As for the program's other requirements, the SA 109 was capable of seating four, although the rear bench seat should be reserved for the less-than-average adult; ride, handling, and braking were aided by the use of a hydropneumatic suspension on all wheels (the previous vehicles utilized the system on one set of wheels only); and the aerodynamic styling, although not ground-breaking, was pleasing to the eye, with its flush door handles, a roof line that dipped at the vehicle's rear, and small side-view mirrors that were set high on the roof line. The interior was done in bright yellow and the gear shift was mounted on the dashboard. The SA 109 could accelerate from 0 to 62 mph in 18 seconds. Coefficient of drag for the final version was 0.21.

GHIA VIGNALE FORD MUSTANG

The Ghia Vignale Mustang was a concept aerodynamic four-wheel-drive specialty car, built on a Mustang SVO platform and powered by a 2.3 liter turbocharged 4 cylinder engine. The three-door, four-seat car had flush glass, a contoured windshield with a single wiper, low-profile aerodynamic headlamps, and a partial belly pan. The side glass had an access portion that could be lowered electrically, a common feature of concept cars dating back many years.

Not extreme in the styling department, the Ghia Vignale Mustang did incorporate a hood scoop, small, aerodynamic side mirrors, flared rear fenders, and a rising door-window belt line to give the vehicle some identity.

ITALDESIGN MAYA

The Maya was less of a futuristic concept and more of a realistic proposal developed with the U.S. in mind. Built around an experimental Ford 3 liter V6 mid-mounted engine, the Maya also represented the type of vehicle that could be produced with contained investment by using bent and stamped sheet metal and an engine and transmission assembled in a module fashion off-line.

The vehicle had good aerodynamics (drag coefficient of 0.28) and a stance that was quite wide at the rear: 2.4 inches wider than the front. The roof was removable and could be placed in the rear luggage compartment. The interior was classic Italdesign with special attention placed on location of controls—on the steering wheel—and a wraparound dashboard that transformed into an armrest upon reaching the door panels. The seats' cushion height could be regulated, and seat-back side bolsters adjusted to the driver's physique.

Additional luggage space was created by situating the spare tire in the rear, thus providing a relatively spacious—relative to other mid-engine coupes—front luggage area.

Two years after the first mock-up appeared in 1984, Ford dropped the project.

ITALDESIGN TOGETHER

The Together was presented at a time when other companies (Renault, Chrysler, Honda, Nissan, to name a few) were experimenting with the concept of a space van; or, in today's vernacular, a minivan. Italdesign stated in its press material that "this architectural layout (the space van) is destined to become a popular trend in the future." Can't argue with that.

To provide substantial interior room while minimizing exterior volume, the Together had a short rear overhang, pedals pushed far forward in the cabin, and a high roof (64 inches). The most significant feature of the vehicle was the seating arrangement. Two or three rows of seats could be created. Aside from the usual two rows of bench seats, an extra two-seat bench folded out in the rear. Multiple arrangements were possible with the rotating front seats and the flat-fold flexibility of the rear seats which created a double bed. The lowering of the body belt line (the point where the window meets the body) on the front doors was significant in that it aided in visibility during city driving.

The dashboard was fitted with an inside and outside temperature gauge, systems-check indicator, and magnetic-card map computer.

LOTUS ETNA

The significant design feature of the Italdesign-conceived Etna was the transparent dome. By encircling the vehicle completely in glass and utilizing very thin pillars, the driver had excellent visibility. The only break in the smooth glass were the two slots just behind the fixed side windows, which provided air for the 4 liter V8 engine, and a second interruption of the glass over the rear deck, where a "cave" was cut out to allow the hot engine air to escape. The interior had a definite driver's feel with all controls push button and slanted toward the driver's position. The driver had the option of using voice activation for controls. The Etna was also fitted with "proximity radar," which warned the driver of an impending collision with a moving object within 250 feet front or rear. Gauges were all analog. The wedge-type body was constructed of Kevlar and carbon-fiber reinforcements. The overall design was extremely production orientated, with practical lines and a comfortable interior. The performance was there also with a top speed of 178 mph.

1984

OPEL JUNIOR

Two-thirds of the Opel Junior's entire length was reserved for the interior. Very short in length—only 134 inches—the Junior still provided room for four occupants.

Features of the vehicle included: a two-piece plastic roof that could be interchanged with either a folding canvas or see-through panorama roof; seat upholstery that could be removed and used as a sleeping bag or ground covers; removable storage cases in the doors; and stereo and loudspeakers that could be removed for portable use. The air vents, connected by flexible bellows-like rubber hose, could swing around in any direction.

The rear seats could be folded forward and the rear gate utilized a "jackknife principle" (the door would fold slightly as it was raised), allowing the hatch to be opened in tight spaces.

The Junior's 1.2 liter engine propelled the car to a top speed of approximately 90 mph. The vehicle had good aerodynamics given its length (Cd 0.31) because of the use of smooth under-body coverings, flush doors and windows, and aerodynamic rocker panel wind diffractors and wheel covers.

PEUGEOT QUASAR

The Quasar was the first of a series of show cars presented by Peugeot at the Paris Motor Show (the others were the 1986 Proxima and the 1988 Oxia).

The Quasar was a compact-appearing two-seat vehicle that had a sloping nose with extensive glass and an abruptly terminated rear. The 4 cylinder in-line twin turbo engine developing 600 horsepower and the four-wheel-drive system were left uncovered and fully visible from the rear.

Inside the cockpit's transparent dome sat a one-piece, nearly door-to-door dashboard supported solely from the central tunnel. The stereo system was mounted directly in front of the passenger. The interior trim was colored in dark blue and red leather. The use of electronics in the interior included dichroic transflective liquid crystals for the instrumentation to provide optimum legibility by day or night. A CRT displayed warning messages and road maps, as well as telex messages.

PORSCHE 928 4-SEATER

The Porsche 928 4-seater was a special 75th birthday present for Dr. Ferry Porsche presented by the Porsche workforce. Completed in just nine months, the 4-seater was built on an extended 928 chassis—10 inches longer—with an upright B-pillar allowing easy entrance for the two extra passengers. The roof line was straightened and lengthened to increase rear passenger headroom, thus creating a quasi-hatchback profile.

The vehicle was powered by the new 4 valve 5 liter V8.

Weighing in at 3580 pounds, the 4-seater was capable of a 0–60 mph time of 6.5 seconds. Top speed was 160 mph. A Daimler-Benz four-speed transmission was utilized. Suspension was altered slightly with harder rear springs and shock absorbers.

Interior amenities included computer-programmed front-seat settings, telephone, alarm system, and Blaupunkt stereo system.

VOLANIS APOLLON

Designer Antoine Volanis, formerly of the French company Matra, designed what might be the most aerodynamic sedan ever in the Apollon. During a period when a coefficient of drag below 0.25 was considered streamlined, the Apollon cut the air with a mere 0.13 resistance. Distinctive sleek features of the vehicle applied after extensive wind-tunnel testing included a high rear deck and an under-body tunnel which ran the length of the car and channeled air exiting the radiator. Vehicle ground clearance adjusted in relation to speed. At speeds in excess of 74 mph, the car automatically lowered to a ground clearance of only 2.7 inches, providing a smooth sail.

The interior consisted of four plush individual seats—two front and two back—with the two front surrounded by a wraparound dashboard. Instrumentation was sparse, with a small boxlike screen located behind the steering wheel. Controls were mounted on the steering wheel. The best high-tech feature of the vehicle was the doors, which opened via an infrared remote-control box. In the case of an emergency, the doors automatically unlocked. The elimination of door handles also improved aerodynamics. A radio guiding system displayed traffic information on a monitor that also functioned as the screen for the rear-mounted camera. The rear passengers were privy to a television and magnetoscope. An anti-collision system alerted the driver to other vehicles in cases of bad weather.

AUSTIN ROVER MG EX-E

The designation "EX" signified exactly what this vehicle was: an experiment. And not just a styling experiment, but a fully operational vehicle.

The base of the MG EX-E was a V6 all-aluminum 3 liter engine placed forward of the rear axle that could motivate the car to a top speed of 170 mph. The sleek vehicle had a drag coefficient of 0.24 and achieved zero front and rear lift without the use of spoilers. The canopy was all glass, with thick supportive pillars sunk below glass level. The side mirrors were mounted high atop the front pillar.

The interior featured a Vehicle Environment Management System (VEMS), which performed a number of functions: Door openings were controlled via a credit card-style key with a driver PIN (personal identification number); ignition was activated by inserting the card into the ignition slot and entering the PIN—this action also automatically activated the seat, mirror, and heat/air conditioning adjustments to the driver's preset requirements; and windshield wipers were automatically engaged when rain was sensed. The information on the instrument panel (speed, fuel level, warning lights, etc.) was displayed according to vehicle condition and/or driver demand. According to circumstances, a head-up display would select limited "priority data" to project. Mounted to the center of the vehicle was the on-board computer and TV screen which provided navigational aid and traffic information assessed via a hands-off cellular telephone link.

BERTONE RAMARRO

The Ramarro, or "green lizard," two-seat coupe was built over Chevrolet Corvette mechanicals. It was the second attempt by Bertone to utilize an American chassis. The first was the Testudo, based on the Corvair. The wheelbase of the Ramarro remained the same as the vette, but the length was reduced about 10 inches. The long nose and chopped-off tail were some of the styling similarities to the American vette. Luggage capacity was limited to a small spot behind the seats since the radiator was housed in the rear over-hang. Bertone took off in another direction with the rounded glass canopy, tinted to hide the pillars. Quite unique to the vehicle was the center-door placement of the door handle. It does appear almost as an afterthought with it set in the side groove. Also atypical in an age of gull-wing and scissor-type doors were sliding doors which were double action, simultaneously opening sideways and forward. The rails on which the doors slid were integrated into the body to make them look a part of the body line.

The interior was clothed in green lizard-skin leather; hence, the green lizard reference. The seat padding ran in a door-to-door fashion over the center transmission hump, which was conspicuously missing the gear shift lever. Instead, the driver changed gears via a dial mounted on the dashboard.

CITROEN EOLE

The most original feature of the Eole was the hinged front wheel covers. Although the style emphasized aerodynamics and the covered wheels were an excellent method for air resistance, a major obstacle arose when turning the vehicle. Citroën solved this problem by hinging the spats covering the front wheels, allowing the cover to open and close via hydraulics linked to the steering system. At high speeds in situations when minimal front-wheel movement was required—as in lane changing—the spats remained closed. The sole non-aerodynamic feature was the large side mirrors.

The interior housed a rail that ran between the front and back seats. This rail could be fitted with various electronic gadgets such as a computer, video game, television, and stereo for use by both front and rear passengers. The transmission was engaged via tactile identification buttons. A portion of the roof over the front passengers was glass. The Eole was also outfitted with the Citroën hydropneumatic suspension that automatically adjusted to load level.

This four-door wagon was based on the mechanicals of the Citroën XM and was machined entirely by computers.

GHIA TSX-4

The Ghia Vignale TSX-4 was a concept sports sedan with the functionality of a station wagon. The TSX-4—Touring Sport Extra 4-Wheel-Drive—nomenclature indicated the vehicle was equipped with an experimental Ford-developed four-wheel-drive system. The low-profile front end had an integral spoiler, radiator air intake, and flush-fitting headlamp unit with full-width light bar—a signature of the production model Ford Sable sedan and wagon. The single-section screened-glass rear tailgate cut forward into the roof panel, hinging at a point above the rear seat back for easier access to the luggage compartment.

The TSX was constructed on the floor pan of a North American Ford Tempo sedan and powered by a transverse-mounted 2.3 liter 120 horsepower engine. Top speed was projected at 120 mph. Drag coefficient was 0.30.

All interior controls were steering-wheel-mounted and the ignition and starter were operated through a high-security, programmable push-button code system located in the center console unit. A television set was provided for rear passengers, and a home computer with the keyboard and visual display unit was built into a special security compartment.

GHIA URBY

The Ghia Urby, a concept design by Ford Motor Company's Ghia Studio in Turin, Italy, was developed to show the interior spaciousness achievable in a relatively short city car. Although it was up to 30 inches shorter than many other cars of the same time period, it could seat four adults in modest comfort, although it's questionable how Ghia came to this conclusion since the vehicle lacks a finished interior. One other unusual feature discovered after examining the photos provided by Ghia were that one side of the vehicle displayed a horizontal door handle mounted directly to the door while the other side featured a handle integrated vertically into the pillar. It's possible that the two photos were taken at different periods during the concept development or that it was a purposely added feature. After all, styling experimentation takes all forms.

The name Urby refers to the vehicle's practicality for urban markets, where space is at a premium. The vehicle's overall length was a minute 139.3 inches, allowing for maneuverability.

PEUGEOT GRIFFE 4

The Peugeot Griffe was designed to commemorate thirty years of cooperation between Peugeot and Pininfarina, as well as give Peugeot an idea for possible future production vehicles. The four-passenger streamlined coupe—a bit more aerodynamic than typical Peugeot coupes—utilized extensive glass for excellent interior lighting. The window-within-a-window scheme, which allowed a smaller portion of the side window to be lowered independent of the full window, was reminiscent of some earlier Pininfarina designs (1981 Quartz Audi Quattro and 1983 Pininfarina Coupe). The model was built from epowood, and thus was not a running prototype.

SAAB EV-1

This 2+2 sports coupe, the only true concept car produced by Saab, featured a roof comprised completely of glass. Because of this, the vehicle's interior absorbed a large amount of heat. To reduce this heat buildup, a continuous ventilation system was created using solar cells for power generation. The removable glass roof over the front seats incorporated 66 solar cells that powered an electric fan in the ventilation air exhaust. An additional feature was the unconventional bumper shields constructed from aramide fiber-reinforced plastic across the entire width of the car. Upon collision, the material would deform elastically and regain its original shape without cracking.

The seats were electrically heated and adjusted fore-and-aft and in height. The backrest was also electrically controlled. Saab also introduced in the EV-1 an integrated belt tensioner which activated within 10 milliseconds of a collision, to reduce the forward movement of the occupant. As another safety-engineered feature, the speedometer was the sole analog instrumentation visible to the driver. Saab determined this as the main information that must not be obscured by the "information noise" produced by less important instruments and signals. Other gauges could be turned on or off manually or automatically, if a warning system came into operation. The headlights were unique in that they incorporated separate light sources for full beam, low beam, and running lights. The EV-1 had a 4 cylinder 2 liter turbo engine that developed 282 horsepower. Top speed was 168 mph.

SBARRO CHALLENGE

The Sbarro Challenge appeared at three different times: the Challenge (1985; pictured here), the Challenge II (1986), and the Challenge III (1987). Only a single copy of the Challenge I and III were produced while five copies of the Challenge II exist. All three versions carried the same uninterrupted smooth line from nose tip to rear and extremely low stance. The Challenge I was a four-wheel-drive vehicle powered by a centrally mounted V8 Mercedes-Benz 5 liter engine. The Challenge I had a sound aerodynamical form allowing a good coefficient of drag of 0.26. Two adjustable rear wings added stability. The doors were scissors-type, opening straight up. Rear visibility was quite poor with the two rear wheel humps and two spoilers limiting window area—but with nary a rearview mirror why have a window at all? A rear-mounted camera and an interior monitor did provide the driver with rearward vision. But with a top speed of 180 mph, rear vision was probably superfluous.

ALFA ROMEO COUPE & SPIDER

Developed by Pininfarina, the Alfa Romeo Coupe and Spider were very typical of the production Alfas of the day, with a simple, light appearance, a radiator grille incorporating the Alfa Romeo logo, and a raised rear-body line. The vehicles were designed to get the best possible result out of common body parts. The idea was to reduce production costs while still developing two distinct vehicles. The doors, front mud guard, rear and front bumpers, and rear and front lights are common to both vehicles. The roof panel on the coupe was made of glass. The interior was unfinished and adorned with a dummy. The cars were quite sleek with a coefficient of drag under 0.30.

AUSTIN ROVER CCV

The CCV (Coupe Concept Vehicle) followed the high-tech Austin Rover MG EX-E, which appeared a year earlier. But the CCV displayed itself as a more practical vehicle. Built over the Rover 800 chassis and suspension, the CCV was a two-door coupe with room for four adults. Drag coefficient was acceptable at 0.27 with the holdover MG EX-E flush glass work. The vehicle also utilized a card-key lock system with door locks engaged via a PIN (personal identification number) and an infrared remote door-locking device. In the interior, controls fell within hands' reach on two small units on either side of the steering wheel. These units housed displays of various vehicle systems including suspension setting, spoiler adjustment, and vehicle environment controls. The center console incorporated the in-car entertainment system, which included a compact disc player and a hands-off cellular phone. The console extended rearward, between the seats, presenting the passengers with a video monitor and remote controls for headphones. All instrumentation featured liquid crystal display but were presented in an analog format supplemented by a digital speedometer.

CITROEN ZABRUS

Taking Citroën BX-4TC four-wheel-drive mechanicals, Bertone created the Zabrus—an attempt to combine comfort, personality, and performance.

Some exterior concepts were holdovers—the same scissors-type doors utilized on the 1968 Bertone Carabo concept were placed on the Zabrus—and the flush glass and bodywork are a Bertone trademark. But the interior was where the Zabrus made a statement. The front seats swiveled around and an automatic seat-adjustment system of infrared cells positioned the seat at the optimum height for each occupant. Convenience and safety concerns divided the instruments into two groups: optical and tactile.

The optical (gauges, etc.) were placed as high and as far away from the driver as possible. The tactile functions (controls, etc.) were all grouped near the driver on a special console.

The compact disc player installed in the Zabrus could store trip information, such as road maps and a list of hotels in the area; of course this information would have to be pre-programmed. The ceiling, too, was unique with its leather mosaic. Why not decorate your car as you decorate your home? the argument at Bertone went. Graphics also dotted the kangaroo-finished leather seats.

IAD ALIEN

The Alien designers had the express purpose of designing a vehicle that visually separated the functional and technical; the functional being the rear compartment housing the running gear and the technical being the front area housing the driver compartment. Mission accomplished.

The driving position was fixed with air bag support in each seat consisting of a multi-chamber diaphragm. The system provided extra support on cornering and also featured an air-pulse system that could aid driver alertness and relieve pressure points during long journeys.

The steering wheel was actually not a wheel, but a two-handled grip mechanism that housed various controls. The turn signals were engaged with the press of a button rather than the use of a lever. The doors locked and unlocked and the engine started by means of an infrared key, which clipped to the vehicle when in use, deactivating steering/gearbox lock and alarm.

The engine and suspension were mounted to a removable chassis sub-frame. Major service could be completed easily and different engine units fitted as required.

ITALDESIGN INCAS

The Incas was a car that couldn't decide whether to be a gull-wing or a flip-top; so it was both. Combining the best of both worlds, the Incas was a mid-engine coupe with three doors and four seats. Entrance into either front seat was performed by flipping up the forward-opening windshield and door unit. Gull-winged rear doors provided movement into the rear seats.

The vehicle design utilized loads of glass—very common in Italdesign cars of its time—and had a stylish profile highlighted by a thick black strip running the width of the car that served as a split between the car's two halves (top and bottom) and also smartly concealed three rear cooling fins.

The interior took a fighter-jet approach with an airplane-style control stick as a steering mechanism which housed the gear shift and controls for heating, windshield wipers, turn signals, stereo system, and cruise control.

The aim of this design project was to create a sports car that could be built with contained investment and the equipment and technologies currently utilized by major car manufacturers.

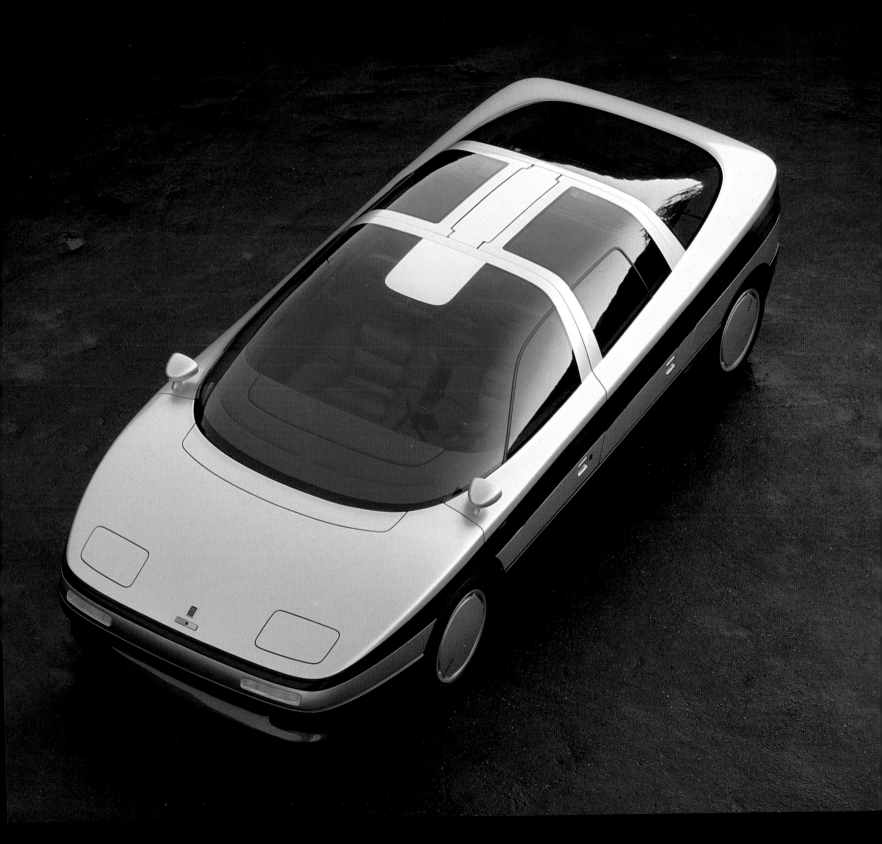

ITALDESIGN ORBIT

The Orbit was built on a Volkswagen Golf Syncro four-wheel-drive platform with a goal of creating a compact space wagon with comfortable seating for four occupants.

To achieve this, Italdesign nixed the typical rear bench seat and replaced it with two individual seats similar to the front; with the center transmission tunnel running the length of the vehicle, this gave each passenger his own compartment. Each seat was equipped with a spring system that adjusted to the shape of the passenger's lumbar region. The seat back was hollowed in the middle to supply ventilation.

The styling was dominated by rounded edges—nothing new for an Italdesign vehicle or for any concept vehicle in the mid-eighties—with gull-wing doors, smooth bumpers, and even a rear high-mount third stoplight for U.S. regulations. The front support pillar (A-pillar) was visually concealed, but the rear pillar was large and slanted in the opposite direction of conventional cars.

The interior contained a symmetrical dashboard that allowed a right- or left-side placement of the steering wheel. Diverging from most Italdesign concepts, only a few controls were mounted on the steering wheel. As with all concept vehicles of the day, the Orbit had the obligatory compact disc player and road map display.

PEUGEOT PROXIMA

This 2 + 2 coupe was a bit on the wild side as styling goes; the nearly nonexistent front and rear overhangs, as well as the unique detached look of the semi-covered rear wheels, attest to that. The second of three pure show cars to come from Peugeot (the others were the 1984 Quasar and 1988 Oxia) the Proxima was powered by a rear-mounted 600 horsepower twin-turbo V6 engine. The Proxima was also equipped with a four-wheel-drive system that activated automatically when an on-board computer sensed rear-wheel spin. Tire pressure was monitored and automatically restored.

The vehicle's interior was replete with techno-gadgets including a navigation system and a rear-mounted camera which displayed images on an interior monitor. A total of five color displays were installed for driver and passenger use. Entrance was facilitated by the forward-pivoting of the all-glass canopy.

VOLKSWAGEN SCOOTER

The Volkswagen Scooter was a slippery (drag coefficient of 0.25) gull-winged vehicle that could top 130 mph on three wheels. Skinned in fiberglass, the teardrop-shaped Scooter had flush bumpers, seamless glass and flush headlights and door handles, and removable gull-wing doors and rear window. The wind-tunnel-honed concept was designed to fill a void between motorcycle and sports car.

The interior housed two multi-toned seats, an unsophisticated instrument arrangement, a radio with cassette, and a removable glove box that could double as a briefcase. The fully operational, 1200-pound vehicle was tested with two engines: a 40 horsepower 1.0 liter and a 90 horsepower 1.4 liter. The latter of the two powerplants, placed transversely and driving the front wheels, motivated the Scooter from 0 to 60 mph in 8.5 seconds.

IAD IMPACT

The Impact was one of three concepts from IAD based on the Ford Sierra XR 4×4 chassis; the other two were the Hunter and the Interstate.

The Impact provided 27 cubic feet of luggage capacity along with an additional 5 cubic feet available beneath the floor area. The under floor was accessible through an electrically operated exterior-mounted stowage door. The spare wheel was also stored in this area on a sliding tray. The tailgate was split, the upper portion operating conventionally while the lower portions opened downward to form a step.

The interior housed four individual seats; the front two were capable of pivoting. A keyboard flipped out of the middle of the dashboard revealing the navigation system. Although not functional, the navigation system's on-board computer would be linked to navigational satellites throughout the world. The computer would also be linked to an on-board engine diagnosis system for ongoing mechanical and electronic vehicle data. Also included in the Impact was a high-tech compact disc system and a not-so-high-tech fabric bag glove box secured by belts.

RENAULT VESTA 2

The Renault VESTA project was proposed by France's Ministry of Industry. Its goal was for the country's car manufac-

turers to produce a vehicle with fuel economy of 94.2 mpg (British Imperial gallon; or 79.4 U.S. gallon). The Vesta 2 was the third and final prototype produced by Renault under this project. The VESTA 1 and VESTA + were the first two vehicles built beginning in 1983. Seven road-going prototypes were built (three VESTA 1, three VESTA +, and one VESTA 2).

Areas of major concern in attempting to achieve the program's fuel economy goal were: rolling resistance, weight saving, transmission, engine, and aerodynamics.

The VESTA 1 did not meet the original goals of 94.2 mpg with its 3 cylinder engine. The second vehicle, the VESTA +, was shortened to 11 feet 7 inches and achieved a drag coefficient of 0.22, but it still did not reach the fuel economy goal. The final prototype, the VESTA 2, did.

The VESTA 2, although based on the Renault 5, utilized mostly new, smaller components. Only a single running prototype was produced. Some of the features of the vehicle were: integral electronically controlled pneumatic suspension with ride height control as a function of speed; electrically controlled cooling system; thin (2 mm) fixed glass (a small portion of side window lowered); lightweight front bucket seats; 11 inch wheels (12 inch were too big and 10 inch too small for the brakes); a twin-choke carburetor with electric regulation which cut off fuel supply as the car decelerated; and extensive use of lightweight magnesium in the engine and transmission. Final figure for the VESTA 2: average fuel economy of 100.5 mpg (British Imperial gallon). At a constant speed of 56 mph, the VESTA 2 achieved 145 mpg (British Imperial gallon; or 122 mpg U.S. gallon). Top speed was 87 mph.

SBARRO MONSTER G

What better name for a road vehicle that utilized Boeing 747 wheels? This bulky, doorless car/truck/sport utility/ conversation piece was designed and built by the inventive Franco Sbarro of Switzerland, father of some of the most unusual vehicles this side of NASA. The Monster G was powered by a 350 horsepower 6.9 liter V8 Mercedes-Benz engine with four-wheel drive. Length was 184 inches and the vehicle weighed 3315 pounds. The base chassis, transmission, and suspension came from a Range Rover. Any and all similarities to the English mark end abruptly there.

Adding to the vehicle's wild aura were the lack of doors—in fact, the entire vehicle was open-air—and the exhaust pipes that jutted out of the hood like sharp bottom teeth in urgent need of orthodontic treatment. The interior was sparse, with a basic instrument cluster and no radio. The cargo area housed a small Honda generator, an additional battery, and a small folding motorcycle. Not to be too uncouth, the Monster G was equipped with Recaro bucket seats.

SBARRO ROBUR

The Swiss designer Sbarro has made a living out of creating the unusual. The Robur is a prime example. Built specifically for a client, the Robur is truly a one-of-a-kind.

The most significant (read: fascinating) feature of the Robur was the set of extra wheels. Not spare tires but two rollers set under the rear of the vehicle, arranged perpendicular to the rear wheels. The extra wheels' function: to aid with maneuvers in tight quarters, especially parking. When needed, the two wheels dropped from the rear, lifted the vehicle's back end, began rolling, and swung the vehicle into place. The action allowed the Robur to park in an area just 10 percent longer than its 120 inch length. Powering the Robur was an Audi 2.2 liter 220 horsepower engine mounted behind the two seats. A hinged flap at the vehicle's rear roof line tilted upward 20 degrees when the brakes were operated. The interior was snug and featured a good stereo system as well as air conditioning.

MATRA P.29

Two spoilers, a partial glass roof, naked front suspension, a narrow front nose, and a 0 to 60 mph time of 5 seconds. Yes, the Matra P.29 was a pure concept car.

The main targets during the design of the P.29 concerned accelerating ability, road stability, and braking power. Accelerating ability was addressed with the weight reduction realized by the use of composite materials and a super-charged 4 cylinder 1966 cc rear-mounted engine. Road stability was aided with the dual spoilers, front and rear. The rear wing adjusted according to the grip of rear versus front axle. The brakes were ventilated discs equipped with ABS. The P.29 was also equipped with full-time four-wheel drive. The vehicle could handle lateral acceleration of 1.2 Gs, about 50 percent better than the average vehicle.

For all its performance goals, the P.29 made a mark more for its unorthodox styling. The front suspension was exposed, while the tires—look closely—were partially concealed with a black cover showcasing a tire-tread design. In combination with a front spoiler that extended the width of the vehicle, a semi-Indy car look arose. But the high rear wing and hatchback look opposed that, creating a design hybrid of sorts: more of a beach-buggy look than a road vehicle.

Technological features included front radar for bad weather, a driver's assistant map, rearview camera, and interior-mounted monitor and permanent controlled and adjusted tire pressure.

BERTONE GENESIS

The Genesis was the minivan for the performance set. Powered by the Lamborghini V12, this people mover could get the kids to school on time without a problem.

The Genesis was 60 inches high, 178 inches long, and had room for five with three rows of seats in a two-one-two seating arrangement. The fifth center seat could be folded and used as a table. The bases of the front seats were actually upholstered wheel arches with the backrest completely separate and attached to the floor. The seat design allowed the front passenger's seat back to pivot around to face the rear passengers. Each seat contained built-in speakers with individual channel selection. Revealing a new twist on door openings, the Genesis' front doors flipped up à la gull-wing, but also had a forward slant due to the hinge placement dead center on the front windshield. The extensive use of glass—typical Bertone—meant that even with the hinge line on the windshield, visibility was not a problem. All controls were located on the center console.

CITROEN ACTIVA

The Activa—and Activa 2—were the test bed for features found on current Citroën models. Although the rear hinged doors have yet to find their way to mass production at Citroën, the hydropneumatic active suspension has found application in current Citroëns.

A heads-up display system which projected vital driving information in hologram form 47 inches beyond the windshield was introduced on the Activa 1 and Activa 2 and was also adopted by the Citroën XM. The Activa also incorporated four-wheel steering, anti-lock braking, and traction control for wheel spin.

The exterior was smooth with an extensive glass area circling the vehicle uniformly, overlapping the support pillars and giving the impression of continuity. The plush interior contained another design touch still to catch the public's desire—yet found on a number of experimental vehicles: a rectangular steering wheel. The vehicle also lacked a gear-shift lever, opting for a console-mounted flat control device.

IAD HUNTER

With a name like Hunter, this IAD concept could be nothing but a sports/utility vehicle. Based on Ford Sierra XR 4×4 mechanicals—the same package as the 1987 IAD Impact and the 1988 Interstate—the Hunter was a rugged open-top (off) roadster equipped with a navigation system and a cellular telephone.

The interior included molded seats and door trims upholstered in weather-proof materials. Those parts of the interior not upholstered were covered with "soft touch" rubberized paint.

The under floor of the Hunter was accessible through electrically operated doors. The spare tire was also stored in this area and mounted to a sliding carrier. The load capacity of the two-seat vehicle was 20 cubic feet with 5 cubic feet beneath the floor area.

The audio system included six speakers, radio/cassette, DAT, and intercom. The DAT/radio cassette system and two speakers were detachable, forming a portable sound system.

IAD INTERSTATE

The most unusual feature of the IAD Interstate might not be a feature at all, but its name. The name Interstate implies something a bit more along the lines of a cruising luxury sedan, rather than a multi-purpose vehicle. With a V6 engine mounted under a soundproof cover, independent coil springs, anti-roll bar, and a minimum ground clearance of 12.5 inches, the 2800 pound Interstate could certainly find a home off-road. The Ford Sierra 4 × 4 chassis used for the Interstate was also utilized for the 1987 IAD Hunter and 1988 IAD Impact.

A tilting glass panel formed the front of the roof and could be removed and stored behind the rear seats. The long doors provided easy access to the three rear seats. Bumpers and all lower body panels were constructed of reinforced reaction-injected molding, providing chip resistance.

The goal of the Interstate, according to IAD, may be as contradictory as the name, the vehicle being "the sort of car which is very much in vogue at the current time and the styling theme is directed at a vehicle for the immediate future."

ITALDESIGN ASGARD

The Asgard sought to cover three areas: performance, safe roadholding, and aggressive styling. The first two were accomplished with the aid of a 200 horsepower engine and four-wheel drive, respectively. The latter was achieved with a round, edge-softening style seen on some earlier Italdesign concepts, like the 1982 Capsula.

The vehicle looked very smooth with side pillars blended into the glass windows, lending continuity to its appearance. The windows even continued down the side of the vehicle, comprising nearly half of the doors. In what was becoming a common feature on Italdesign concepts, the Asgard had a service area located between the rear door and covered rear wheel, housing various gadgets.

The floor was raised, allowing room for three passengers in the front as well as back. There were six regular seating places in the Asgard: Next to the driver's was a bench-type for two and in the back three separate seats. Two additional children's seats in the rear faced rearward and could be folded away to provide luggage space. The controls were all within easy reach of the driver, including the automatic gear lever mounted in the center of the dashboard.

ITALDESIGN ASPID

If the Aspid has a family resemblance to the Italdesign Aztec, it is more than coincidence: They are primarily the same car. Taking the basic "one-box coupe" design (as it's known to car designers) of the Aztec spider, Italdesign conceived a coupe.

The difference between the vehicles began at the belt line—the line surrounding the car where the glass and body meet—the Aspid eliminating the gull-wings and adding a glass windshield hinged at the front. The roof was split down the middle, allowing the passenger and driver sides to be opened independently. The side doors opened out as they did on the Aztec. The tail of the coupe was higher with an adjustable spoiler. A gap between the spoiler and the car body created ventilation of the mid-mounted engine.

The interior was still comprised of two well-defined symmetrical compartments divided by the central tunnel. And yes, the "service centers" on the car's side, containing various gadgets (tools, air hose, etc.), remained.

ITALDESIGN AZTEC

The four-wheel-drive Aztec offered a distinctive interpretation of the spider design with a two-passenger cockpit divided into two symmetrical sections with individual windscreens. To enter the vehicle, the doors swung open as with a typical car, then the individual windshield units flipped up, displaying a semi-gull-wing look.

On each side of the vehicle, the smooth sheet-metal surface was interrupted by a "service center." The right side housed the digital gauges for the cooling liquid and brake levels, a removable thermometer, a gauge that showed the level of the air filter's remaining filtering capacity, a 12 volt DC outlet, and a hydraulic lift. On the vehicle's left side were fuel filler and relative level gauge, two compartments containing an electric torch, a compressor to increase tire pressure, and a fire extinguisher. The headlights were pop-up type, but their block configuration ran in the face of aerodynamics and styling.

The interior featured two instrument panels, one for each occupant. The driver's instrument panel provided information on the vehicle while the passenger's instrument panel held a navigation system that displayed information such as traffic density, route details, safe following distance, and a weather forecast.

With slight modifications, the Aztec went into limited production early in 1991.

IAD ROYALE

Intended for the business executive or the would-be entrepreneur, the IAD Royale may not have broken new ground in exterior styling, but its interior certainly pampered the passengers.

Unique to this interior and developed jointly by IAD and Philips B.V. were centrally mounted rotary key pads. These revolving remote controls (duplicated in the front and rear) replaced traditional controls for three systems: in-car entertainment, information and navigation, and business.

The entertainment section of the rotary pad enabled both front and rear passengers to control sound levels and choice of sound source: radio, cassette, or compact disc player.

For information and navigation, the rear passengers were provided with two televisions with individual headphone attachments. A television screen for use with a navigation system was integrated into the dashboard. Front and rear hands-free telephones were installed. And what business car is complete without a facsimile machine incorporated into the back seat and a lap-top personal computer.

Additionally, the Royale, based on a stretched Subaru body, incorporated composite headlamps, plus an LED screen integrated into the tail-lamp configuration that displayed the car registration number as well as other information relevant to road safety.

MICHELOTTI PURA

The translation of the Italian word Pura is "pure." The only wonder about the vehicle's name, then, was pure what? With the top put away, it meant pure fun. With the top on or off and the engine winding out, it meant pure high-speed fun. This concept from the now-defunct Michelotti of Italy was built over an Alfa Romeo 4 cylinder 1.8 liter turbocharged engine set midship. Wheelbase for the Pura was 97 inches and total length 142 inches. Slotted Ferrari-like air intakes for the engine were set in the top of the rear fender. Vehicle weight was only 1436 pounds for this two-seater as body construction relied heavily on composite materials and carbon fiber. The glass canopy slid back to allow entrance and could be stored away—in a garage, not anywhere on the vehicle—to provide wind-in-the-hair driving. The interior was unsophisticated, with the usual array of instrumentation placed where one would expect to find it. The really strange piece of design on the Pura was the periscopelike rearview mirror. The assumption must have been that with such a high rear end, normal placement of the mirrors would have been ineffective. This new placement was merely inventive.

PEUGEOT OXIA

The Peugeot Oxia, named after an area on the planet Mars—Oxia Palus, which lies at latitude and longitude zero—was created by stylists and engineers at Peugeot's La Garenne research center in France. Powered by a 680 horsepower V6 transversely mounted engine behind the passenger compartment, the Oxia was capable of a top speed of 187 mph.

The vehicle's exterior was formed of a carbon fiber, Kevlar, and epoxy-resin composite bonded to aluminum honeycomb and sheet panels giving the vehicle light weight and rigidity.

A communications center, equipped with a personal computer, a display screen, and a combined radio-telephone, managed the air-conditioning system and provided travel data and navigational information. The computerized air-conditioning system ensured that the selected temperature and airflow were maintained regardless of external conditions. When the car was stopped, the system drew power from 18 solar cells to maintain airflow through the passenger compartment. Weather and traffic conditions and information on the route or destination were accessible via the radio-telephone.

PININFARINA HIT

The most striking feature of the Pininfarina HIT (an acronym for High Italian Technology) was the set of four square headlamps along the front of the vehicle. The white bumpers were integrated into the body, providing good aerodynamics with the vehicle achieving a drag coefficient of 0.29. The red and green body stripes reflect the colors of the Italian flag. Some of the body lines are similar to the 1991 Audi Quartz by Pininfarina, but the HIT was much more smooth and less extreme. The engine hood, front fenders, and bumper arose from a single mould and were hinged at the front. The interior contained very easy-to-read instrumentation with a grouping of analog gauges against a black background. Jutting out from the middle of the dashboard was a large control panel containing the vehicle controls. The seats, also done in Italian red and green, were contoured with a shoulder harness for each front seat. The platform and body were designed fresh, which indicated that Pininfarina had become more than simply a coachbuilder.

RENAULT MEGANE

With seats that look as if they were stripped right out of a 747's first-class section, the Renault Mégane was, if nothing else, a comfortable ride. And with a V6 3 liter turbocharged engine and a top speed of 160 mph, it was a quick one, too.

Features of the Mégane included sliding doors—two on each side that popped away from the car body slightly, then slid back over their respective quarter-panels—and a front passenger seat that spun around to face the rear passengers. The rear seats could recline and the rear window could slide back, allowing more rear head space. The single front windshield-wiper blade was concealed under a panel until engaged. The bottom of the trunk could slide out for easy luggage loading. The fully adjustable driver's console included the steering wheel, analog gauges, two video monitors (relaying information from the two rear-mounted cameras), and easy-to-reach controls.

The Mégane was a fully operational concept incorporating much advanced equipment like navigation system, electronic air conditioning, and two roof-mounted and retractable rear video screens.

UTAH 7

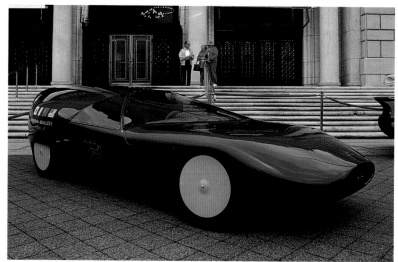

UTAH 9

UTAH 10

UTAH 12

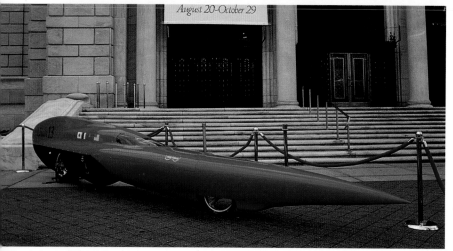

UTAH 13

COLANI UTAHs

The designs of Luigi Colani have always been a bit eccentric; the UTAH experiments were no exception. Emphasizing what Colani termed bio-design, the UTAH vehicles lack anything resembling a straight line. For a straight line was boring to Colani and he frequently commented about the unimaginative designs of the major manufacturers. For Colani, the UTAHs represented a wake-up call for car designers worldwide.

The UTAH 6 was a concept Volkswagen Rabbit two-seater mid-engine sports car study. The 1300 cc Rabbit engine was mounted in a mountain-racing chassis. The fiberglass bodywork utilized a "wing door" for driver and passenger. Length was 13.1 feet, width 6.7 feet, and height 2.9 feet. Weight was approximately 1500 pounds.

The UTAH 7 was a four-seater with a drag coefficient of 0.18. The engine was a water-cooled 49 cc Fichtel & Sachs two-stroke engine. Body material was fiberglass, reinforced plastic, and plexiglass. The vehicle weighed approximately 1300 pounds.

UTAH 9 was an experimental electric aerodynamic (weren't they all?) vehicle, very atypical of the average electric experimental car. Length was 13.7 feet, width 4.6 feet, and height 2.9 feet. The vehicle weighed a modest 1600 pounds and used the Citroën 2CV chassis.

UTAH 10 was a super-streamlined low-profile concept vehicle with a 148 horsepower 500 racing, water-cooled 3 cylinder Honda two-stroke engine.

UTAH 12 was a transport and concept truck based on a Mercedes-Benz chassis. Powered by a 15,070 cc diesel V8 engine, the UTAH 12 was capable of 91 mph top speed. Coefficient of drag was 0.38. The total length of the vehicle was 20.5 feet. Width was 8.2 feet and height was 12.1 feet.

UTAH 13 was a two-wheeler with a 1300 cc turbo-charged nitrous oxide-boosted 350 horsepower engine. The vehicle attempted to break the motorcycle speed record.

UTAH 6

FERRARI MYTHOS

Built on a Ferrari Testarossa chassis, the Mythos was characterized by the huge side air intakes, which funnelled cool air to the vehicle's mid-engine V12. The car's steel frame was wrapped with doors and body panels of carbon fiber. The two-seat coupe had very aggressive styling, with a rake windshield, plunging nose, and a stance eight inches wider in the rear than the front. The coefficient of drag was only 0.37, but record aerodynamics was not the goal of the Mythos project. Although the car had an aggressive look, excessive ornamentation was limited. Just look for the door handles. They were placed under the body side indentation created by the huge side air intakes. The rear spoiler raised and lowered as much as 12 inches. A front lip spoiler also acted as a downforce. Both were activated at speeds of 62 mph and retracted at 44 mph. The slots under each headlight were cooling-air ducts.

The interior design was highlighted by simplicity. Two symmetrical units on each side of the steering wheel housed the controls. The aluminum pedals moved to suit the driver who was secured with five-point seat belts. The rearview mirror was integrated into the top of the windshield.

FORD GHIA BEBOP

A car that looks much like its name: the Bebop. The word, defined as a jazz music with complex harmony and highly syncopated rhythm, fits nicely with this design around a Fiesta chassis.

The pickup truck-like Bebop was a five-color montage of white, yellow, turquoise, blue, and violet specifically designed for maximum impact and effect—as well as safety: The bright yellow front could not be missed in the rearview mirror of another driver.

A drop-down tailgate, designed to lie flush with the load floor, was reinforced to support loads extending the length of the flatbed. Behind the two-seat cab was a bulkhead which could be removed in two parts. The upper half, a large moulded bubble window, could be either latched open for extra ventilation or taken out completely. The lower half was a rigid load retainer which could also be removed after the window to create an open back.

Extra roof lamps with aerodynamic covers could be detached with the extended power cord, allowing six feet of hand-held use.

GHIA VIA

The Ghia Via was the first car in the world to incorporate a unique fiber-optic headlight system. Wafer-thin lamp clusters were positioned at the base of the windshield for maximum efficiency. Each consisted of nine separate fiber-optic units illuminated from a central source, providing illumination equal to a much larger halogen system. The headlamps could also be programmed to operate as fog lights or spotlights. The rear spoiler lay flush with the bodywork at low speeds, but was deployed automatically by an onboard computer to provide downforce as speed increased. The design of the rear windows allowed stale air from the interior compartment to be extracted through a small slot. The roof of the Via had a removable targa-type center section made of photosensitive glass to protect the occupants. The instrument panel used advanced fiber-optic lighting techniques to create a floating effect for the instrument needles. Controls more frequently used were arranged so they could be operated by the driver without removing his hands from the steering wheel.

G. POLLMAN DIE LIMOUSINE

If nothing else, Die Limousine may have been the largest cabriolet ever. The four-door behemoth was 200 inches long with a 122 inch wheelbase. Power originated from a compact 6 cylinder engine whose flat top comprised a large portion of the front hood. Addressing the inherent safety risk in open-top vehicles, Die Limousine was equipped with a roll bar which released in 0.3 seconds after a serious impact. Space saving took special attention with the design of inner-gripping disc brakes and an antenna integrated into the A-pillar.

With the poor rear visibility, the vehicle featured a sort of curb radar, informing the driver via a display behind the steering wheel of an impending curb crash. Instrumentation was analog and the steering center housed an air bag. Many of the controls and knobs were·ergonomically designed with finger-size curvatures for easy use. This bulky sun-vehicle was not without unique luggage capacity either. A large tray above each rear wheel slid open to provide extra cargo space, and a long, narrow compartment just above the rear exhaust was the ultimate alternative to roof-mounted ski racks.

IAD VENUS

The British design firm IAD took a very unique approach to wheel treatment in the Venus by enclosing the tires in pod-like compartments. When the Venus is first viewed, it appears as though the tires are the round pods when, in actuality, the pods simply encase the tires, providing a barrier to road spray and enhancing the low-slung, race car image.

Powering the 43 inch high Venus was a mid-mounted in-line 4 cylinder 16 valve engine. The doors were scissors-type, swinging up to allow entry and counterbalanced for easy operation. The two seats were stationary, while the steering wheel and pedals were independently adjustable.

Forward nighttime vision was enhanced with an infrared camera supplementing the halogen headlights. Rear vision, impeded by the low seating position, was aided by a rear-mounted camera that transmitted images of the vehicles just passed onto a color television screen.

MATRA M 25

The French firm Matra chose a method of celebrating its 25th anniversary that many car enthusiasts would love to try: it introduced a truly high-performance concept vehicle. The two-seat M 25 (Matra 25th anniversary) was a pocket rocket built over a diminutive 136.5 inches of length. The rear-mounted 197 horsepower 4 cylinder 1.8 liter Renault turbo engine propelled the vehicle from 0 to 60 mph in a mere 4.5 seconds. Top speed was 160 mph. With a body constructed of carbon fiber and Kevlar placed over aluminum honeycomb, light weight (only 1550 pounds) and rigidity were guaranteed. Inside the M 25 were two bucket seats with four-point seat belts and modest instrumentation located on a small pod behind the steering wheel. A small area behind the seats was available for luggage. Overhang on the M 25 was slight—almost nonexistent in the rear—and a huge spoiler was perched on the rear deck. The roof was completely glass—a section was also removable—and a single large wiper serviced the entire windshield.

ITALDESIGN KENSINGTON

If it looks like a Jaguar and sounds like a Jaguar, chances are, it's a Jaguar. No exception here. The Kensington was a tame experimental car (tame compared to some earlier Italdesign concoctions) based on a Jaguar platform meant to be clearly identified as a Jaguar.

Goal achieved.

The main difference between the Kensington and the production Sovereign Jaguar was the aggressive, wide stance of the Italian version with mud guard-type bumps over the headlamps continuing to the front pillar and a high, muscular rear end. Some structural changes were made by replacing the two lateral gas tanks in the trunk with a 100 liter tank in the center of the luggage compartment. The production Jaguar also had a longer front overhang and a shorter rear overhang (due to the modified gas tank). Much care was taken to continue the smooth lines inside and out, with very soft and curved shapes in the interior.

The original mechanicals of the Sovereign remained unchanged: V12, 295 horsepower engine mated to a three-speed automotive transmission.

ITALDESIGN PROTO C

The Proto C was proposed for the small sports car market. The great attraction of the Proto C was its flexibility; with only small modifications to bodywork, the vehicle could become a coupe, cabrio, or speedster. Length was a skimpy 160 inches. The Proto C could be fitted with two engines: a 1 liter 60 horsepower powerplant or a more powerful 6 cylinder. Front-wheel or four-wheel drive were also options.

Features of the Proto C included automatic reception of information broadcast regarding traffic conditions, an air filter system which cleaned interior air, a solar roof panel capable of charging the battery, and a heat collector which kept the interior warm when the car was parked outside on cold nights. In the event of an accident, the steering column and the seat belts would retract automatically. On the environment-friendly side, the engine would shut down automatically during a traffic stop of more than five seconds, then restart instantly when it was time to move.

ITALDESIGN PROTO T./TL

The research model Proto T./TL was presented in two steps. The first was in 1989 at the Frankfurt Motor Show as an epowood model simply designated "T" and then at the 1990 Geneva Motor Show with fully finished interior and extended name: Proto T./TL.

The four-door sedan designed by Italdesign for the Spanish automaker Seat was characterized by a smooth, sloping profile with very high rear end, and extensive glass area; the base of the windshield sat far forward and the base of the rear window continued almost completely to the rear. The roof glass had varying degrees of transparency that could automatically adjust to outside light intensity. The flush glasswork was a recurring theme in Italdesign vehicles.

The interior boasted a wraparound style incorporating the door panels, dashboard, and windscreen. Aside from the classic analog instrumentation were two small monitors that showed the driver the images from the camera placed where the rearview mirrors normally were. A third camera could be placed within the line of taillamps to assist in tight maneuvering. The car started via a magnetic card instead of a metal key.

PININFARINA CNR E2

The Pininfarina CNR E2 was developed in cooperation with Fiat Auto and Alfa Lancia on behalf of the Italian National Research Council. The project's goal was to design a medium-class sedan with excellent aerodynamics. The vehicle achieved a coefficient of drag of 0.193—with flush door handles and half-covered rear wheels—while still providing a roomy interior capable of seating five. The vehicle had low weight (1165 pounds) and was powered by a 1.4 liter engine. Top speed was 125 mph.

The CNR E2 was a follow-up to the CNR experimental form designed in the Pininfarina wind tunnel in 1978.

PORSCHE PANAMERICANA

To commemorate the 80th birthday of Prof. Dr. Ferdinand "Ferry" Porsche, the concept Panamericana was designed. Built on the chassis of the Porsche Carerra 4, the two-seat convertible had a removable canvas roof and body panels composed of both fiberglass and carbon fiber. A zippered rear window and canvas top were used with the top incorporating two symmetrical bubbles for head space. The concept took only seven months to complete.

The most unusual feature of the Panamericana was not any part of its body styling (although the carved wheel wells were a bit unique) but rather the tires. A special tire-tread design incorporating the Porsche logo was developed by Goodyear Tire specifically for the Panamericana.

RENAULT LAGUNA

Wind-in-the-hair driving to a "T." The Renault Laguna, without a windscreen, was a pure roadster. A sliding tonneau cover replaced the traditional roof, but its sole purpose was to cover the car when not in use.

The most distinctive feature of the Laguna—aside from its striking styling—was the pop-up roll bar, or roll hoop. The two hoops were hidden from view behind each of the two seats. When a computer sensed a collision or a change in the angle of the vehicle—the car beginning to roll over—the bars sprung up. Activation time was one-tenth of a second. Additional features on the Laguna were gull-wing doors, carbon fiber and Kevlar outerskin, and an audio visor worn by the driver and passenger to protect the eyes and enjoy the stereo system. The seats were fully integrated into the body floor.

This fully functional vehicle was powered by a 2 liter turbo mid-mounted engine capable of propelling the Laguna to a top speed of 155 mph.

CITROEN ACTIVA 2

Following the Activa 1, the Activa 2 was a more production-like four-seat two-door coupe. The hydractive suspension fitted to the vehicle modified its attitude according to speed to achieve the best aerodynamics (headlights automatically adjusted to compensate for the change), raised the vehicle at rest when the doors were opened to make passenger entry and exit easier, and provided active anti-roll. The anti-roll suspension component of the Activa 2 kept the vehicle flat while negotiating severe curves through an interaction between a computer monitoring speed and steering angle and the hydraulic suspension system.

Another feature of the vehicle was the heads-up display system which projected vital driving information on the windshield. The interior also included a multi-function screen connected to a computer. The screen monitored the twenty-four safety functions and notified the driver if any problems were detected. This system was developed in the Activa 1 and was used in the production Citroën XM. The Activa 2 also eliminated the transmission lever and replaced it with a set of buttons on the center console.

The screen could also assist with navigation by displaying route information and notifying the driver via a synthesized voice. As with most navigation systems, limitations existed; with the Activa 2 system, navigation assistance was confined to the streets of Paris.

ADC MULTI-PURPOSE VEHICLE

Built by Automotive Development Centre (ADC) on a Rover Metro chassis, this vehicle could be expanded into a wide range of multi-purpose vehicles. La Petite Famille was designed for the needs of a small family with bike rack, removable seats, and integral fold-down child's seat. The Sunrider was aimed at the younger buyer with the capability to carry windsurfer, water skis, and related sporting equipment. The Country appealed to those who had more rugged, outdoor activities in mind with its addition of mud flaps and a dirty-boots storage area. The Metropolis was a vehicle for the city dweller. It featured anti—curb-scuff wheel trim and a cellular phone. The Specialist was directed towards the "photographer" who needs to get to a wide variety of locations carrying a multitude of equipment. The final version was named La Femme. The features of La Femme included a breakdown communicator/telephone, mini hair dryer, power steering, large driver and passenger's sunvisor with mirror, and parking ticket holder.

ALFA ROMEO 164 PROTEO

The initial conflict facing the designers who were planning the Proteo was whether to design it as a coupe or a spider. The consensus: do both. With this decision made, the engineers at Alfa Romeo then designed a roof that retracted into the rear luggage compartment, thus covering both options. The process began with the rear window section sliding back and then the rear compartment sliding open, allowing the window to swing in. The glass roof followed the rear window into the compartment as the cover slid back into place; automatically. When in place above the occupants, the glass roof was designed to allow the driver to control the amount of light let into the cabin. The glass was also a "solar control," cutting solar energy entering the cabin by 40 percent. This special glass was developed by PPG Industries. The car's two bucket seats were set very low to the ground and each slid back as the doors opened. The seat belts were integrated into the seat.

The Proteo was powered by an experimental 260 horsepower 24 valve 3 liter DOHC engine and equipped with both four-wheel steering and four-wheel drive. Also on the high-tech end, the Proteo featured an electronically controlled suspension system which automatically chose between two settings: sport and comfort. The driver could have elected to override the system and engage the sport mode manually through a cockpit switch. Nighttime vision was handled easily with six powerful pencil-beam headlamps set into the Proteo's one-piece carbon fiber nose.

AUDI AVUS QUATTRO

The Avus Quattro obtained its name from the Avus race-track in Berlin, so it is no wonder that the car has such racing car-like attributes.

The top racing-like feature of the Avus Quattro was probably its powerful engine. The mid-mounted 12 cylinder 6 liter power plant generated 509 horsepower from a unique configuration: two banks of four cylinders were arranged at an angle of 120 degrees, and the third was positioned upright in between the other two. Audi designated this the W12 configuration. What the W12 provided was a compact engine with excellent power. Top speed from the four-wheel-drive machine was 210 mph with 0 to 60 mph in 3 seconds.

The most visually striking feature of the Avus Quattro was the hand-moulded, all-aluminum body and over-size tires—a definite reference to the Auto Union racing machines of the 1930s. The scissors-type doors opened simultaneously forward and upward. The side-view mirrors were mounted high on the door frame and an air duct on the heavily glassed roof fed air to the engine. Glass also covered the engine bay. The cockpit, lined in leather, wood, and woollen textiles, was unadorned with high-tech instruments, only a simple, unobtrusive compact grouping of analog gauges set directly before the driver.

The dimensions of the Avus Quattro also attest to its power emphasis: length 176 inches, width 79 inches, and height a mere 46 inches. Rumors are circulating that Audi may build a limited number for public sale. Price: $1 million each.

AUDI QUATTRO SPYDER

The main purpose behind the construction of the Audi Quattro Spyder was to demonstrate the potential of aluminum (used for both the body and tubular frame) for weight saving in car design. The Audi designers were given the target of building a high-tech vehicle that could be duplicated in series production without a profligate price tag: i.e., around or below $60,000. Concern for the environment was addressed in the vehicle also, the use of the lightweight aluminum cutting fuel consumption and emissions. The aluminum was also recyclable.

But for all its concerns about price and the environment this two-seat high-performance vehicle still had a 2.8 liter V6 engine placed transversely behind the seats that theo-retically could propel the car from 0 to 60 mph in under six seconds with four-wheel drive. Top speed was predicted at 155 mph.

The closed Spyder could be converted quickly into an open-air car. The glass roof was provided with a solar panel and could be removed and secured on top of the engine hatch. On hot, sunny days the solar cells provided enough current for the fan, providing permanent ventilation of the interior when the car was parked. The interior featured specially developed sport seats, a dashboard of advanced plastic material, and an aluminum gear lever. The Quattro Spyder was 46 inches high, 166 inches long, and weighed 2420 pounds.

BERTONE EMOTION

The press material distributed on the Emotion states: "It bears no innovative elements or revolutionary concepts, the Emotion is a charming car."

All cars should be lucky to look so "charming."

Built over Lotus mechanicals, the Emotion had a front end tailored to redirect the airflow downward over the radiator at low speeds, then upward to prevent lift at high speeds. At the rear, a mobile aileron adjusted itself in relation to speed. The roof design was interesting, a small triangular section being the only non-transparent section. All pillars except the thin front supports were hidden under the flush glass. Dimensions of the Emotion were: length 162 inches, width 76 inches, and height 43 inches. The car was originally just a design mock-up, but eventually became a running prototype.

BERTONE NIVOLA

The Nivola utilized the Chevrolet Corvette ZR-1 5.7 liter V8 engine. But the similarities to the American vette end there. Rather than using the Corvette plastic body, the Nivola was fashioned from traditional sheet steel. The styling also departed from the vette. But that's fairly obvious.

The Nivola featured a light, retractable roof that stored above the engine compartment. To avoid the usual luggage problems associated with rear-mounted engines, Bertone utilized the doors as a storage area. The outer panels of each door hinged at the bottom, opening with a handle located in the front mirrors. A special briefcase was designed to fit into each compartment. The interior upholstery of purple and green featured massage vibrators in the cradles to soothe the legs during long journeys. All instrumentation was digital. The pop-up headlights were distinct because each unit comprised two individual tiny lights set on top of each other. The taillamps were extraordinarily small—although with concept cars, nothing (or everything) should be termed "extraordinary"—and recessed into the rear section. The Nivola was also equipped with hydro-pneumatic shocks which controlled ride height.

The name Nivola comes from the nickname of Italian racer Tazio Nuvolari. The yellow paint was also a reference to Nuvolari, who wore a trademark yellow racing sweater.

Bertone also developed two other vehicles on U.S. mechanicals: the Testudo (1963) and Ramarro (1984).

BMW E1

The electric-motor BMW E1 was one of many cars developed with the zero-emission requirements of California in mind. Designed as an alternative for city driving, the 2 + 2 E1 combined good aerodynamics with compact exterior shape and sufficient interior space.

Special design measures were applied to the body structure and occupant zone to minimize the effects of typical city traffic accidents, such as sideswipes or nose-to-tail collisions. For example, a protective knee pad was incorporated below the facia. An electric heating system which used waste heat from the battery and motor, whenever possible, helped keep additional energy consumption to a minimum. The E1 was entirely suitable for cold-weather use without needing any fossil fuels and could be pre-heated under programmed control while the battery recharged. The windshield reflected infrared rays, so that excessive heat could not build up inside the car in hot weather.

The E1's body was a mix construction of aluminum frame and plastic outerskin. Should the vehicle reach mass production, the plastic elements could be manufactured to a large extent from material recycled from other BMW cars.

BMW Z1 STUDY

As the name suggests, it was just that: a study. The 2 + 2 seat touring coupe utilized the BMW Z1 chassis with the four-wheel-drive system of the BMW 325iX, but never progressed past the wood, plastic, and plaster mock-up stage. The "funmobile," as the press material dubbed the vehicle, would be capable of crossing difficult terrain; "a kind of alternative vehicle for hunters," the company went on to say.

The hatchback wagon was finished in deep green and had a roof luggage rack. The seating position was well back towards the rear wheels—as it was in the production Z1—and the hood appeared extremely long. Note the high placement of the side mirrors, set well up the A-pillar.

CITROEN CITELA

The Citela was an electric town car with an interchangeable and recyclable body. Combining its diminutive length (less than 120 inches) and electric operation, the Citela was one of many concepts introduced in the early '90s to combat air pollution and urban crowding.

Featuring a modular construction, the base unit of the Citela contained all of the running gear, while the detachable body could be removed and changed to accommodate different body style. The vehicle had a range of 130 miles on a single charge and a top speed of 70 mph. Each minute of recharge time gave one mile of range.

The interior was compact (that follows the compact exterior), providing room for three adults and one child. The rear wheels were three-quarters covered and placed closer together than the front wheels, aiding in the vehicle's maneuverability.

G. POLLMAN FAMILIENSPASS '91

Quite a few features set the Familienspass '91 (Family Fun '91) apart from the average commuter car. The color combination—turquoise, purple, and yellow—is certainly attention-getting even during these days of fluorescent four-wheelers. But the color was only one reason the Family Fun was atypical. The wide-bodied vehicle had short overhangs—not too unusual—but the convertible system consisted of venetian blind-looking laminated flaps that folded together just above the rear window. Not totally new, but interesting nonetheless.

The interior seat layout was conventional in front, but the two rear seats angled inward, forming a V-shaped storage area from the rear end through to the sides of each seat. Further features included tinted double glass, knee bolsters, air bags, an electrically adjustable child's seat, and a removable communications unit complete with compact disc player and telephone and telefax hook-ups. As with the 1989 G. Pollman Die Limousine, the Family Fun '91 was equipped with a curb alarm, making those tough parking exercises a bit easier.

IAD MINI MPV

The IAD Mini MPV was just what its name implied: a scaled-down version of the popular minivan. Built within a relatively small exterior package, the Mini MPV provided considerable interior space with the use of short front and rear overhangs. The central driving position in combination with the extensive glass area provided excellent visibility, along with allowing for a relatively unfrustrating drive in both the United States and England, being neither right- nor left-hand-drive.

Up to six people could ride in the vehicle, or luggage space could be increased by removing seats or folding flat the rear bench seats. Additionally, the driver's seat and second-row passenger seats revolved 360 degrees or tilted to form picnic tables.

The front and rear wipers revolved in a 360-degree sweep, cleaning both the windows and, in the case of the front wiper, the headlamps as well.

IAD/RAF MINI-BUS

This Mini-Bus was produced in a joint effort between the Latvian manufacturer Riga Automotive Fabrika (RAF) and IAD of Great Britain. After years of producing a minibus for the Eastern European market, RAF wished to increase its export market through production of a technologically more advanced vehicle. This goal led to the hook-up with IAD and the production of the IAD RAF Mini-Bus concept, designed to give potential investors an understanding of the type of vehicle planned.

The new production launch is scheduled for 1997 in a new RAF facility. The initial vehicle concept was a nine-seat bus with a forward-mounted eight-valve 2.3 liter engine. Both right-hand and left-hand driver could be accommodated. Wheelbase was 2950 mm.

ITALDESIGN NAZCA C2

The Nazca C2 was the second Italdesign vehicle of 1991 based on BMW 850i mechanicals. The other was the Nazca M12. The modifications to the Nazca C2 consisted of upgrading the engine, reducing weight, and making a few aesthetic tweaks. The C2 designation alluded to the Group C sports cars.

The V12 engine was tuned to increase horsepower to 350 from 300 in the Nazca C2. Weight was reduced by approximately 221 pounds. Styling changes were summed up by Italdesign: "more aggressive."

Specific exterior changes were a widening of the track, redoing of the front end and mud guards, and the addition of two rear spoilers. These changes were necessitated by the need to improve roadholding, negative lift, and engine ventilation, because of the greater power delivered. The signature BMW kidney grille that cooled the radiator was kept. The doors were opened in the traditional manner while the windows flipped up, gull-wing style. New carbon-fiber seats were installed to reduce weight further. The headlights were placed lower to a point actually illegal for everyday driving. But with a top speed of more than 185 mph and a 0–60 mph time of 3.8 seconds, the Nazca C2 was far from an everyday car.

ITALDESIGN NAZCA M12

The Nazca M12 was one of two Italdesign concepts produced in 1991 over BMW 850i V12 mechanicals. The other was the Nazca C2. Although the familiar BMW kidney grille and insignia are present, BMW did not commission the work.

Built with carbon-fiber and light alloy components, the Nazca M12 weighed in at around 2431 pounds. The carbon-fiber frame was a single piece connected to a tubular frame which held the central engine and the steel architecture, which, in turn, supported the glass dome. The car body was composed of the two doors and of a front and rear part, each consisting of a hood/trunk and mud guard in a single piece. The glass dome—providing 360 degrees of vision—incorporated gull-wing windows. The doors opened separately and more traditionally. The window automatically rose when the door was opened. The side windows could be removed, thus converting the Nazca M12 into an open-topped car.

Most dramatic of the Nazca M12 was the styling, comprised of very round shapes and uncluttered surfaces. Designed as more than an exercise, the Nazca M12 may find its way to limited production.

LOTUS M200

The Lotus M200 had a very similar look to the production Lotus Elan from the wheel tread up to the body waist line—in fact, the M200 was based on the Elan chassis—but from the waist line up, the car differed strikingly. Added were an aerodynamic roll-over bar with adjustable trim tab, individual low-profile aeroscreens, high-downforce rear wing and deeper front bib and spoiler for increased downforce and stability, and fixed-reflex headlamps with removable lens. The passenger compartment was divided by a bar which ran at windscreen height.

The car stood on 17 inch magnesium-alloy wheels. The interior was lined in "Lycra"/leather trim, the instrument graphics were set in contrasting black and white, and the floor mats incorporated a tire-tread pattern design.

MERCEDES-BENZ C112

The most recent addition to the string of Mercedes-Benz concept vehicles was the C112 introduced in 1991. The car was developed, as were the predecessors—the C111, C111-II, and C111-III—as a research laboratory on wheels, testing such features as active and passive safety, ABS, ASR, automatic temperature control, radar distance monitoring, and tire-pressure control.

The gull-winged C112 implemented an actively variable aerodynamic system which adjusted the rear aerofoil. Under normal conditions, the aerofoil remained at rest. But at extreme conditions, where additional roadholding was required, the aerofoil moved upward and rearward within a tenth of a second. The aerofoil also aided in braking by providing downward force on the wheels.

The Active Body Control (ABC) utilized in the C112 featured a computer and sensor system that monitored vehicle pitch, roll, and lifting, and automatically adjusted suspension.

Passive safety was addressed by a reinforced cab with integrated roll-over bar. In the case of a roll-over accident, the usually servo-assisted gull-wing doors automatically opened.

MERCEDES-BENZ F100

The F100 concept represented a new research area for Mercedes-Benz: the minivan market. Even the color—purple—was a fresh attempt for the German make.

The front-wheel drive (also quite new for a publicly displayed Mercedes) F100 seated five in 1-2-2 arrangement. That is, the driver sat dead center front, followed by two rows of seats. The middle driving position was chosen for its safety; the middle of the vehicle being the safest in an accident. All seats could be removed save the driver's seat. The doors opened out, as do conventional car doors, but then swiveled out. The doors even incorporated part of the roof and platform, allowing the driver easier access to the middle seat. The rear doors on both sides slid out and back. Two cameras and a monitor increased rear visibility, while a traffic-monitoring radar system warned the driver before changing lanes or helped detect obstacles on the road. A solar collector on the roof stored enough energy to ventilate the interior.

Although the F100 made a stir upon its introduction, and rumors of its production were rampant, the vehicle remains just a concept.

OPEL ECO 2

The Opel Eco 2 was a response to the need for a more environment-friendly vehicle. This meant producing a car that consumed less fuel and expelled less emissions. The Eco 2's 1.6 liter 8 valve engine produced 40 percent less carbon dioxide emissions than the average German car. Locating the catalytic convertor close to the engine meant the convertor reached operating temperature quickly and reduced cold-start emissions. Utilizing long piston strokes and a compression ratio of 10.8:1 also reduced fuel usage.

Another special technical feature of the Eco 2 was its five-gear transmission which had an extremely long fifth gear (ratio 0.63). This allowed economical driving at low speeds.

Aerodynamics were increased by using a smaller radiator (long-stroke engines could function with fewer cooling ducts), covering the rear wheel housings, and adding a rear spoiler.

Another factor in fuel consumption—tire rolling resistance—was addressed with the use of low-resistance tires developed by Goodyear. The special rubber compound and weight-optimized design of the tires reduced rolling resistance by 40 percent.

PININFARINA CHRONOS

The Chronos was built over a shortened Lotus Omega floor pan on Lotus Omega mechanicals. Although initially not a running model, it eventually became one. One of the main features of the Chronos was its shape, which promoted downward force.

Another notable feature was the transparent canopy. When removed, the roof panel fit on the rear deck behind the seats, still leaving a fair amount of room for luggage.

The two-seat Chronos was powered by a 377 horsepower 3.6 liter twin turbo-charged 24 valve engine mated to a 6 speed gear box. Top speed was 190 mph.

The vehicle's body was made of Kevlar, saving some 440 pounds over the weight of the Lotus Omega four-door.

RENAULT SCENIC

The Renault Scenic reflected a need of customers with families—according to Renault—who wish to travel "out of the ordinary" and are attracted by the idea of a "cocoon" of a car. The design revealed this theme quite effectively.

The features of the Scenic included minuscule exterior dimensions (163 inches long, 75 inches wide, 72 inches high), while accommodating five seats, all bucket. The Scenic had a safety structure with a double floor containing the luggage compartment—actually capable of holding twice that of a production Renault Espace minivan—and a vertical-flow air-conditioning system whose channels formed members that ensured the rigidity of the passenger compartment and freedom for the designer by eliminating dashboard air vents.

The Scenic was equipped with permanent four-wheel drive, a multi-valve 2 liter engine with variable valve timing, and an automatic transmission in which the selector lever was replaced by a small keyboard.

The driving position, recalling that of a helicopter in its arrangement—spacious and uncluttered—was equipped with a navigation aid and a driver-drowsiness detection system. To further emphasize the travel orientation of the vehicle, an imaginary map was outlined on the carpet. Directions to utopia, possibly?

VOLKSWAGEN CHICO

The Volkswagen Chico was a hybrid-powered compact 2 + 2 vehicle designed for use in densely populated regions and the areas surrounding them. The vehicle allowed for automatic switch-over from a combustion engine to an electric motor. The spark ignition engine worked mainly during acceleration and at speeds more than 32 mph. The 6 kW electric motor was utilized during phases when the vehicle was being driven at an almost constant speed in town traffic.

The two-door hatchback Chico was only 126 inches long and 64 inches high. In order to provide easy entrance and exit, a four-joint door hinge was developed combining the elements of a sliding door with those of a wing door. The driver was supplied with information via two displays. There was a liquid display on the dashboard which supplied the usual data—on road and engine speed—and a head-up display supplied destination-tracking information.

VOLKSWAGEN FUTURA

The development of the Integrated Research Volkswagen Futura was a result of the ecological concerns coming to the forefront of automotive design in the early 1990s. Fitted with a 1.7 liter high-compression gasoline engine with direct fuel injection, a mechanical supercharger, and a compression ratio of 16 to 1, the engine could produce an ultra-lean fuel/air mixture to reduce emissions and increase fuel economy.

Further technological goodies of the gull-winged Futura included a sensor warning system that notified the driver via a dashboard light when an obstacle or car in front of the vehicle was too near. An on-board navigation system advised the driver of the best possible route to his or her destination. This navigation system, combined with an electronic all-wheel steering system which moved the front and rear wheels automatically, enabled the car to park itself with a touch of a button. Ecological concerns tied in with navigation in terms of the fuel saved in avoiding traffic jams.

Another Futura feature was a noise-cancellation system. Microphones in each head restraint picked up the ambient noise heard within the vehicle and played it back through the loudspeakers out of phase to cancel the noise. Known as anti-noise or noise cancellation system, it reduces the noise inside the passenger compartment by about 50 percent.

VOLKSWAGEN VARIO I & II

Although both vehicles used the same surname, the similarities beyond that were very few. In fact, take away the common name and all these two vehicles had in common was a chassis; both were based on the VW Golf Syncro four-wheel-drive floor pan. They were not even produced by the same group; the Vario I was designed in-house at Volkswagen, while the Vario II was constructed by students at the Art Center College of Design in Switzerland.

The Vario I was a true harkening back to the days of the beach buggy; a definite fun-time vehicle. Bodied in aluminum and strengthened components, the Vario I had as much rigidity as the VW Cabriolet. The most striking visual feature of the vehicle was the interior—a montage of yellow, red, blue, black, mauve, etc., set the theme for this leisure vehicle. The fabric was, of course, weather resistant. Some features of the Vario I were: a personal stereo that could be detached from the dashboard and played on the beach (or grass, or office, or . . .), an overhanging tinted cover that swung down to help eliminate sun glare on the instrument panel, and grab handles for quick entrance and exits.

The Vario II, left in the hands of design students, ended as a much more aggressive-appearing vehicle. The four-passenger coupe/spider—coupe for the front two passengers, spider for the rumble seat occupants—featured a transparent removable roof that covered only the front two seats. A single bar running from the top of the windshield down behind the front seats created a T-top look when the glass was removed. The two rumble seats were accessed with the aid of a step hole cut into the side body. The interior was a little more modest than the Vario I, with the traditional upholstered bucket seats. Instrumentation consisted of four round gauges set in a semi-circle behind the steering wheel.

INDEX